# Evaluating Curriculum Proposals

## A CRITICAL GUIDE

DIGBY C. ANDERSON

A HALSTED PRESS BOOK

CROOM HELM LONDON

JOHN WILEY & SONS
New York

©1981 Digby C. Anderson
Croom Helm Ltd, 2-10 St John's Road, London SW11

British Library Cataloguing in Publication Data

Anderson, Digby C
    Evaluating curriculum proposals. – (Croom
Helm curriculum policy and research series).
1. Curriculum change
I. Title
375'.006        LB1628        80-41177
ISBN 0-7099-0248-4


Published in the U.S.A.
by Halsted Press, a Division of
John Wiley & Sons, Inc., New York


Library of Congress Cataloging in Publication Data

Anderson, Digby C
    Evaluating curriculum proposals
    'A Halsted Press book'
    Bibliography
    Includes index.
    1. Curriculum planning – Evaluation.
2. Educational Research. I. Title.
LB1570.A638        375'.001        80-23324
ISBN 0-470-27075-6

Printed in Great Britain by
Biddles Ltd, Guildford, Surrey

CONTENTS

For Judith

# EVALUATING CURRICULUM PROPOSALS

# FOREWORD

Much curriculum research has been concerned to present itself as 'science' — either in the interests of establishing a factual basis for connecting techniques of curriculum construction to the characteristics of learners and learning environments, or with the aim of putting forward empirical justifications for doctrines about desirable classroom activities. This view of curriculum research is being increasingly challenged. Despite a rapid growth in the sophistication of quantitative research procedures and remarkable developments in the data handling capacity of computers, 'scientific' approaches to curriculum research have failed to establish their credentials. Though serving some limited purposes, they have not helped us significantly in confronting central issues of what should be taught and learned in our schools.

In this book Digby Anderson diagnoses the problem in a new and illuminating way, and points to the kind of reconceptualisation that is needed if curriculum research is to justify itself as an activity with practical and theoretical importance. He does this by renewing, within a framework based on close acquaintance with modern phenomeno-logical sociology, the antique concern of philosophers such as Aristotle with the rhetorical arts and their connection with the moral conduct of human affairs. Founding his arguments on a detailed analysis of the texts of research-based curriculum projects, he shows that, though curriculum writers often seem to be unaware of the fact, their presen-tation of research is deeply rhetorical. He teaches us how to recognize and analyse these rhetorical usages when, as teachers or theorists, we try to evaluate the worth of materials and proposals. He shows how the notion of 'curriculum analysis' can be deepened to make it more than a response to the categories of judgement that writers of proposals themselves enunciate or imply.

Further, he demonstrates that this deeper notion of curriculum analysis must lead us to the conclusion that 'there is not research-free-of-practicality. That there is not one sure and boundaried "it" — 'the real thing'. What curriculum research yields as an activity is a raw material for rhetorically constructed claims, and it is only in this guise that research becomes tangible and open to scrutiny. There is no avail-able 'objective fact' behind the 'story'.

Neglect of this fact, or refusal to countenance it, provides one reason — perhaps the main reason — why much curriculum research has failed to address the needs of teachers. In trying to create a spurious objectivity for itself it has set up a false boundary between the 'expert' and the 'inexpert' and deprived itself of the capability of helping teachers translate general ideas into the particular contexts of classrooms.

These may seem, at first sight, to be difficult ideas. But, as the later chapters of the book make plain, they can lead us back to the 'common-sense' that an overly 'scientific' construction of research has obscured and show how the gulf between theory yielded by research and theory of use to the practitioner can be bridged. This is, in the end, a very practical book. It should be read by all teachers who want to make better judgements about what they should be teaching, and all researchers who are looking for a better sense of what is worth investigating, how and why.

THE EDITORS

# ACKNOWLEDGEMENTS

For much of the period in which this book was written I was working with Wes Sharrock of the University of Manchester. No partnership was ever more unequal. I and many others owe him more than is ever apparent from citation. The basis of my work owes much to the influence and example of David Marsland of Brunel University. Michael Macdonald Ross and Rob Waller of the Open University are two of the rare people doing analysis of this kind. They have both taught me more than they realised. Sections of the work have profited from discussion with Bob McCormick of the Open University, Gwydion Thomas of Ealing College of Higher Education and Peter Barnes of the Open University.

I also acknowledge the support of the Leverhulme Trust and the Nottinghamshire Local Education Authority and its director James Stone; of Henry Fowler, Nick Spencer, Elizabeth Perkins of Nottingham University and of Mary Pearson and Gillian Deave who patiently and swiftly typed the manuscript.

As the references in the book are brief, I would like to acknowledge the pervasive influence of the ideas of Harold Garfinkel (UCLA), the late Harvey Sacks (UCI) and Dorothy Smith (OISE).

Bill Reid, the series editor, initiated the book and was quietly supportive during occasional periods of doubt. But none of these people are in any way associated with the opinions expressed or responsible for errors, looseness and other shortcomings.

DIGBY C. ANDERSON,
University of Nottingham

# 1 THE PROSPECTIVE TEXTUAL EVALUATION OF CURRICULUM PROPOSALS

## A Critical Approach to Curriculum Innovations

This book is concerned with the written curriculum proposals produced by agencies of curriculum innovation such as the Schools Council. Those who wish to criticise or evaluate these books of proposals generally ignore the fact that they are written. They abstract from the book its 'ideas', or 'topic' or 'argument' or 'proposal' or 'research' and criticise or evaluate that. Some, especially in discursive reviews of books, discuss a general area of curriculum concern and refer to the book as it relates to this area. Both kinds of people may cite actual excerpts from the book but usually only to *illustrate* general points. Crudely, a textual criticism is the opposite of such approaches. It is concerned to analyse the 'ideas' or 'topic' or 'argument' or 'proposal' or 'research' of a book as it occurs in the written text and to treat cited excerpts analytically rather than illustratively. It tries to start with the text and the points that it makes are made in response to issues generated while reading the text. That does not mean that knowledge of the world outside the text is not used to understand, analyse and criticise the text. It means that such knowledge is used as a response to issues in the text rather than as a way of selecting issues from the text. It further means that the text is evaluated on its own. The evaluator places himself in much the same position as a well-informed lay reader. He does not rely to any extent on special knowledge about the subject the text addresses, or about the circumstances in which the project produced the text. Nor does he necessarily read all the projects' texts and accompanying material. A textual analysis of a curriculum text also addresses the text as well as the ideas. More precisely, it addresses the interrelationship of the two. The textual analyst is interested in how the text constructs and orders the ideas that the reader discerns. In particular the evaluator-reader is interested in how the text produces any plausibility, significance or other merit he may discern. This is done by close attention to the text. The question is: 'How close is "close"?'

In two ways the analyses in this book are not as close as they should be. First, as is explained in Chapter Two, the intention is not to *do* a definitive textual analysis of the curriculum texts examined but to use texts to generate analytic tools. The texts are treated unscrupulously to derive approaches, concepts and methods for textual analysis. The book is then a demonstration rather than an analysis, but it is arguing that others should do analysis with the methods it demonstrates. Therefore the methods used in the chapters are meant to be examples of how to do a textual analysis of curriculum materials and, like all such examples, they have been tidied for demonstration purposes. It is hoped that anyone undertaking an analysis of a curriculum text 'for real' would be far more rigorous than the demonstrations and far less concerned to make the quick, dramatic conclusions necessary in demonstration. For, in general, books are not good places to *do* textual work. First such work needs to cite huge chunks of the analysed text and this citation not only elongates the book but encounters copyright problems. In this book, for instance, I have had to include only tiny fragments of five curriculum texts. To have included the books themselves would have made this book seven or eight times as long. And even then the analysis would have been 'out of context' for many of the texts examined are parts of a package. Secondly, analysis itself is massively boring. Book readers will be interested in the 'results' rather than the 'working' which may be particular to the case analysed. Thus, for this book, the results are methods for those who wish to address curriculum proposals in a prospective and textual way.

The book is not then 'about' the five curriculum texts and should not be taken as criticism of them. Not only does it not concern itself with them *per se,* but it has nothing to offer their producers. It is not about writing curriculum proposals but about reading them. It is not suggesting changes in the ways that curriculum innovators work and, as far as I can see, its methods would be of little interest to such innovators. Nor is it suggesting that teachers should stop trying curriculum innovations and retire to armchairs for deep analysis.

Quite simply, though, it notes that for good or ill, whether the innovators like it or not, whether the method books approve of it or not, much practical evaluation of curriculum proposals *is* done by *reading parts* of those proposals. Most method books seem unconcerned to help that evaluation-by-reading. This book is an attempt to repair their high-minded omission.

At the time of writing and to the author's knowledge, this is the first book to venture into this area. Obviously the work of such a venture should not be to restrict but to open up new analytic possibilities. In consequence I have not tried to tidy the 'results' — that is the methods of analysis — into a neat scheme or conclusion but prefer to see them as the first of many devices which are open for others to collect. Also in keeping with the tentative nature of the venture, I have not sought to underwrite the methods by extensive references and have frequently used the first person. For it is far more important that critical readers of curriculum texts should address the texts themselves in a sustained way than that they should become linguisticians or rhetoricians. Nor should they think that they are confronted with a solid impersonal established technique – 'textual analysis' – when all they are reading are an individual's suggestions.

One criticism of the curricular innovators which is implicit throughout this book is that they lack a sense of proportion. They do have ideas, tips, and materials for teachers which may be useful, but they present themselves as offering overall perspectives on 'subjects' or children. Their conclusions are out of all proportion to their research and knowledge. It is not that they do not suggest that teachers *develop* their ideas. It is that both explicitly, e.g. in their titles, the number of school years, children etc., they aim to encompass, and in their rhetoric, their glossiness, their confident style, their alleged legitimation by research, they claim a scope, a solidity, a surety, an authority and a novelty which is out of proportion to their displayed research work. Somehow no explicit avowal of humility, no amount of loud deferment to teachers' knowledge, reduces this. Indeed it may be part of it.

In this book I *explicitly* claim no such solidity, surety and authority. I have tried to write in such a way not to claim it *implicitly,* by rhetoric.


## Textual Criticism and other Treatments of Curriculum Innovations

Throughout the sixties and seventies various curriculum projects suggested changes in the matter and methods used in English schools. Proposals were put forward for innovation in science teaching, the humanities, religious education, environmental studies, counselling and a host of others. One of the issues which confronted the projects was the evaluation of their materials and methods in schools. Evaluation was, and still is, a matter of controversy. Munro, for example, contrasts two positions on evaluation:

The first which emphasises measurement and prediction is committed to pre-specification of effects (or 'behaviours') and has been termed the 'classical', 'traditional', 'objectives', 'industrial', 'engineering', or 'agricultural-botany' model by its detractors, and the 'experimental', 'scientific' or 'operational' model by its advocates. The second model emphasises meaningful description in interpretation and is concerned to note emergent effects as evaluation proceeds. It has been called the 'illuminative', 'responsive', 'consensual', 'participant observer', 'analytic-judgemental' or 'social-anthropological' model by its advocates but has not yet been suitably stereotyped by its detractors.[1]

The conflict between these two positions was not particular to the evaluation of curriculum innovations but at least recalled major disputes about approaches to education especially in the fields of management[2] and planning and in the use of behavioural objectives.[3] In turn these were related to the methodological and paradigmatic uncertainty and controversy which the social sciences in general suffered during the latter part of the sixties. The 'illuminative' position was, at least in part, a response to the awareness that evaluating educational change is often evaluating social change and consequently subject to the same difficulties.

But although they differed in many respects, the 'illuminative' and the 'experimental' evaluators both emphasised the scrutiny of actual educational change. They were concerned to try out innovations and, one way or the other to monitor their effects. They understood different things by 'effects'. For some these were pre-specified experimental effects; for others the opinions of cooperating teachers; for others their own sensitive observations; for others ensuing processes. All, however, consistently saw evaluation as connected with trial. The products of the curriculum innovators were to be evaluated during or subsequent to trial.

The receivers of curriculum innovators were, of course, teachers, education students, administrators, researchers and indirectly pupils. All these people had to make their various minds up about aspects of the innovations. Some of them were invited by the innovations to teach different matters or to use different methods; others at least to envisage teaching differently; others to think about the objectives of schooling in a new way and others to study the innovations themselves. Insofar as these people had to 'make up their minds' about the innovations, they too had to do some *evaluation*. For some of them such evaluation could be done along roughly the same lines as those taken by the innovators. They could *try out* the new curricula and, one way or another, see 'if they worked'. But others either could not or did not need to work this way. They practised an armchair evaluation, in which they *read* the curriculum innovation and based their judgement on the reading and their 'experience'. Certainly many students 'evaluate' this way. Equally certainly, so do many teachers. For they cannot *try* everything that people suggest to them. They must at least sift the suggestions which are made in order to decide which ones to try. Researchers and book reviewers also evaluate much of the time in this way. This sort of evaluation, *prospective evaluation* is a necessary and useful part of the total evaluative process though it has received less attention from evaluation commentators than trial methods.

Most notably Michael Eraut has addressed it in 'The Analysis of Curriculum Materials' in which he offers teachers a sophisticated check list procedure for evaluating whether curriculum innovations are relevant to their needs. Eraut's method is based on a scheme for the abstraction of important items from the curricular text and also includes methods for the training of 'curriculum analysts' in workshops. A small section of the scheme is as follows:

PART 2     DESCRIPTION AND ANALYSIS OF
           THE MATERIALS

2.1        *Description of Pupil Materials*

2.1.1      Describe the content of the material, using any of the techniques listed below that seem appropriate.

            Listing major topics; titles or groups of chapters; chapter headings; sub-chapter arrangement; recurring themes; topics listed in the index.

            Sampling the material by selecting typical or important sections and describing their contents at a detailed level. Indicating in quantitative terms the relative emphasis given to different aspects of the subject matter.

2.1        Describe the presentation form of the material, and relate it to the various categories of content.

2.1.3      Describe the pupil exercises or tasks that are included in the material; and indicate how frequently each type of task occurs and how the tasks are sequenced and/or repeated.

2.1.4      List any explicit statements on pupil assessment; and note examples of tests or assessment schemes (indicating both the nature of any specific assessment instruments and the structure of the assessment pattern as a whole).

2.1.5      List, summarise or describe any statements of

purpose, aim or objectives included in the pupil material.

2.1.6            List and estimate the frequency and significance of directions to the pupil to refer to his teacher or to use special or relatively scarce facilities.

2.1.7            Where there is more than one physical resource, indicate the inter-relationships between them in terms of cross-referencing, sequencing and repetition, both of content and of pupil tasks.[4]

I have used the term 'abstraction' above and it is a key one, for we see that the traditional method for handling curriculum books employed both by trial and prospective evaluators is to treat them as if they contained 'points' or 'topics' or 'arguments' or 'evidence' or 'perspectives' or 'methods'. The curricular book, very much like books on other educational or social matters, is regarded as some sort of *receptacle* which contains *ideas*. These ideas are then *taken out* and examined. The examiner, be he teacher, student, book reviewer or whoever then evaluates the idea. He finds that it would or would not work, is good or bad, interesting or boring, sound or speculative, relevant to his own problems or not, etc. This is a reasonable way to treat the curricular book but it is not the only way. For the curricular book is not a collection of 'naked ideas';[5] it is not even a sequence of naked ideas. It is a book. And curriculum books, like most education and social science books, are written, not in equations, but in natural language.[6] Moreover, the choice of book format means that the argument is ordered in a conventional way with sections or chapters, titles and so on. When the reader finds a curriculum book persuasive, good, relevant or in some way convincing he should be alert to the possibility that its plausibility may derive from its bookish as well as its argumentative character.

The notion that the organisation of words in speeches could generate plausibility was, of course, the central notion of classical rhetoric. Rhetoric is no longer a popular subject, but at least we still use words such as 'convincing' of novels, fiction films and so on. Such things also have the power to influence our behaviour and affect our emotions. We also acknowledge that rhetoric can play a part in verbal and written propaganda. I shall suggest that certain sorts of rhetoric are very much part and parcel of curriculum texts, and that, in consequence, a prospective evaluation of curriculum texts should attend to their textual as well as their curricular features for the two turn out in practice to be deeply interrelated. I shall suggest that the things which make a curriculum text at least prospectively attractive include the way the authors characterise themselves, the way they *present* their evidence, the way they quote children's talk, the way they construct lists and a plethora of other features. Every teacher knows that good and interesting lessons derive as much from the way the lessons are presented as from any merits of the 'original' materials or subject matter, yet there is perhaps a reluctance to see that the same is true of curriculum projects which are allegedly based on research. Much as practitioners abuse researchers, they still tend to over-estimate the distance between their arguments and those of daily life. I shall show that the curriculum research project books are deeply, and I believe, inescapably, involved in presentational and rhetorical as well as evidential and logical work. This does not mean that it is wrong to judge them on their 'ideas' alone. It is, however, difficult to do so and even when it can be done it produces an unbalanced criticism and assessment of the curriculum project in question. A criticism and assessment which takes into account the textual features of curriculum projects is what is meant by the title of this chapter, 'Prospective Textual Evaluation'.


**Areas of Enquiry**

One objective of this book is then to help the armchair curriculum critic to *read* critically rather than simply *assess* critically the various curriculum innovations currently on offer. But it would be disingenuous to suggest that my interest is in curriculum texts only or *per se.* Curriculum texts are of special interest to those who wish to examine the rhetoric of academic argument not only because they are in natural language and have all the features of suggestion and allusion that natural language exudes; not only because they are in book form and contain all the presentational devices common in books; but because they point up several prominent issues which arise in many contemporary academic arguments.

First, most of the curriculum projects of the sixties and seventies were both research projects and books. Put another way, their members were both researchers and authors. In the books the authors tell the story of their *own* research. They present a 'version' of that research. They 'edit' the research. There are, it is well known, shelves of books which both tell one how to do research and lay down standards for doing and criticising research. There is considerably less attention given to the issue of how to judge 'edited' research. Yet 'edited' research is the sort of research which is more and more produced. The sort of research which the curriculum projects present is just not amenable to textbook research manual standards and the teacher, student, administrator or researcher who tries to apply such standards will find the greatest difficulty in so doing. The sort of research presented in curriculum texts needs special methods and standards of criticism, ones which are designed for its edited nature.

Secondly, curriculum texts are self-confessed practical texts. They are not only designed to be read by practitioners but to help practice. As such they typify at least one sort of applied research. And a lot of research done in the universities and other research centres is allegedly 'applied'. Obviously one way to judge 'applied' research and to evaluate 'practical' books is to apply and practice them respectively and see what happens. But in the case of the armchair or prospective evaluator this is not possible. He needs standards and methods to help him say which research and books *will* be practical or at least have enough of a chance of doing so to be worth trying. Once again, with the exception of such work as Eraut's and Schwab's, the prospective critic looking for methods to evaluate the practicality of suggestions in texts will find little assistance. Most general books on method in education research do not even address such questions.

Thirdly, curriculum texts are good examples of quasi-academic arguments. Like many suggestions in public policy, in management, in social welfare and elsewhere they clearly have *some* basis in evidence but are not the necessary outcome of evidence; they clearly have affinities with 'logical' and 'scientific' argument but are not the inexorable working out of such argument. One must hold on to this notion tightly. These suggestions, such as the proposals for curricular change, do not become 'ordinary' commonsense, 'worth no more than an individual teacher's musings', or invalid simply because they are not 100 per cent 'scientific'. At the same time they are manifestly not 100 per cent scientific. They are quasi-scientific. How does one judge a quasi-scientific argument? Once again the method books do not rush to our help.

Fourthly, because the curriculum projects are 'practical' and quasi-scientific and because they are established to produce books as well as research, they tend to rely to a considerable extent on *borrowed* perspectives, facts, and methods. Significant parts of their arguments are not established by them but cited from other work. Since many of the readers are not academics and the discipline origins of the cited matter are very varied, problems can emerge. For it is simply the case that the conventional rules of citation are not adequate to help the reader in these (and I shall suggest most other circumstances). How does the reader judge the worth of proposals based on arguments, facts and perspectives beyond his reach?

Fifthly, the reader who starts to read in a rhetorically oriented way starts to notice features of curriculum texts which are less easy to classify. He finds appeals to his emotions; he notices measured phrases; he feels himself directed on one of many possible argumentative paths, lifted and lowered at the author's will to certain levels of generalisation; confronted with paired categories such as problem-solutions; enticed by models of pupils and teachers which are not quite models but not yet metaphors. His critical fire is drawn in certain directions by the author's discrimination of possible controversy, and at other times held in abeyance as the author writes in such a way as to indicate his point is not yet fully made. He finds points come over forcefully, but when he tries to fault them they are hedged about with hesitation and qualification. In short, he finds that he is reading a text and being persuaded (or not) by a text. But the method books only tell him how to evaluate, criticise and judge a disembodied argument.

Curriculum texts are then a useful focus for exploring certain rhetorical features found in the sort of academic text which is preceded by research, allegedly practical, quasi-scientific, strategically dependent on borrowed matter and rhetorically ornamental. Since these five characteristics are common to many policy and planning documents both within and outside education, this study of curriculum texts may have wider applications than simply to curriculum texts.

The book centres on discussion of these five areas and illustrates them by studies of four curriculum projects: *Moral Education in the Secondary School,*[7] *The Humanities Project,*[8] *Religious Education in Primary Schools: Discovering an Approach,*[9] *Health Education Project 9-13,*[10] and one Schools Council 'research study', *Mass Media and the Secondary School.*[11]

## Notes

1. R.G. Munro, *Innovation: Success or Failure?* (Hodder & Stoughton, London, 1977), p. 1.

2. M.W. Apple, 'The Adequacy of Systems Management Procedures in Education', *Journal of Educational Research*, No. 66, (1972) pp. 10-18.

3. M. Macdonald Ross, 'Behavioural Objectives — A Critical Review', *Instructional Science*, Vol. 2, (1973), pp. 1-52.

4. M. Eraut, L. Good and G. Smith, 'The Analysis of Curriculum Materials', University of Sussex Education Area Occasional Paper Nos. 2, (1975), pp. 104-5.

5. I.A. Richards, *The Philosophy of Rhetoric*, (Oxford University Press, New York, 1965), p. 5.

6. J. Schwab, 'The Practical – a Language for Curriculum', *School Review,* Vol. 78, No. 1, (1969).

7. Schools Council Project, *Moral Education in the Secondary School,* (Longmans, London, 1972).

8. Schools Council/Nuffield Humanities Project, *The Humanities Project: an Introduction,* (Heinemann, London, 1970).

9. Schools Council, *Religious Education in Primary Schools: Discovering an Approach,* (London, Macmillan, 1977).

10. Schools Council, Health Education Project 9-13, *Think Well, An Introduction and Food for Thought,* (Nelson, London, 1977).

11. G. Murdock and G. Phelps, Schools Council Research Study, *Mass Media and the Secondary School,* (Macmillan, London, 1973).

# 2 PERSUASIVE CURRICULAR PROPOSALS

## Introduction

The object of this book is to make a collection of some of the features in curricular texts which may influence teachers, education students and others towards accepting the suggestions made in such texts. More precisely, the features I am interested in collecting are to do with the way that the text is written and published, rather than with, say, its relevance to the concerns of a teacher. Obviously, one way for teachers and others to judge curricular proposals is by scrutinising them for relevance, perhaps by setting up a list of the characteristics of the proposals and comparing it with a list of their own concerns and circumstances. Michael Eraut has suggested a series of ways in which this kind of 'Curriculum Evaluation'[1] may be done. But in deciding whether or not a curricular text is relevant to a set of needs and circumstances, the reader has to form an impression of that text. He must decide what it is, in fact, proposing, what evidence it has to back these proposals up, whether the authors know what they are talking about and so on. Now, I have already argued in Chapter One that such impressions are not the result of a purely 'logical' process. For curriculum texts are texts as well as curriculum proposals. And *I,* certainly, have yet to see the curriculum text which even tries to set up a remorseless logical syllogistic argument. The texts that I have seen follow a quasi-logical pattern. They use what Aristotle calls enthymemes[2] ; while their conclusions do not come out of nowhere, while they are not just the fancies of the authors, no more are they the inescapable and inevitable results of the axioms and evidence. For example, the statement in the curricular proposal *Moral Education in the Secondary School:*

> The members of the . . . Project believe that our principal adult responsibility is to help boys and girls to live well — live well in the sense that they learn to care and choose. We believe this *as a result of* a four-year study of secondary school pupils' needs.[3] (my italics)

raises the issue of exactly how the proposals in the text can be the 'result' of the research. Increasingly, curricular proposals do follow a period of research and are displayed 'as the results' of that research.

While I would not want to suggest that there is no relationship between the proposals and the research, I am sure that, to start with, the proposals are not the results *only* of the research and that they are not *logical entailments* of the research data.[4]

The term 'quasi-logical' when used to describe the arguments and proposals of curricular texts is, however, unfortunate in that it draws attention only to what their arguments and the proposals are *not*. While it is important to be aware that rigorous logical standards *cannot* be applied to curricular texts, that curricular texts are *not* like sums, that 'as a result of' does *not* mean 'entails', we would wish to know what standards *can* be applied to curricular texts, what curricular texts *are* like and what 'as a result of' *does* mean. Clearly the arguments in curricular texts work, more or less successfully, and equally clearly they do not work one hundred per cent 'logically'. How do they work? What is persuasive in them?

I shall argue that they work, at least partly, by a number of persuasive devices or features and, in the rest of this book, show off some of these devices. The collection shown is by no means complete and the object in showing it is to add one more sort of research tool to curriculum analysis. For if these persuasive devices are crucial to the working of curricular arguments, then evaluation of and research into those arguments needs to include attention to them. It is important to note that I am not suggesting these devices account totally for the acceptance and rejection of curriculum proposals, but nor am I just adding 'a few more things for researchers to look at'. If these devices do characterise curricular documents then they alter the overall character of those documents. They mean bluntly and simply that curricular texts based on research are as much rhetoric[5] as science and need to be examined as such.

For some the revelation that curricular proposals are not remorselessly and totally 'logical' provides the opportunity to see them as the result of societal processes. They are the outcome of the deliberations of social individuals and forces. They are, perhaps, ideological rather than logical. Whatever the possible merits of these lines of enquiry, they differ from this investigation. For they involve turning attention to the study of the actions and events which precede or follow the actual proposal: whereas this investigation does not use the revelation that the text is not 'logical' as a reason for seeking to explain its production and acceptance by other factors *than* the text. Rather it looks for other factors *in* the text. As we shall see, some of these turn out to be 'social' in that they concern such things as the relationship of author and reader and in that one of the author's tasks is to describe the social processes of the curriculum research. But these emerge as products of the attempt to grapple with the text itself. While it would be silly to claim that these social observations are 'the result of' grappling with the text in the sense that any grappling would necessarily lead to these same observations, the use of the text does control gratuitous theorising. Thus those who would look elsewhere than the text for explanations of it seem to have the whole social world to choose from, whereas this investigation only looks outside the text if the text *seems* to warrant it.

This emphasis on the 'text and only the text' means that I approach the curriculum texts which I investigate with no privileged knowledge. I do not know how they were produced. I have not any knowledge, nothing to reveal about the secrets behind the documents. Whilst this may disappoint the reader it has at least two advantages apart from that of 'textual control' suggested above. First the reader is in almost[6] the same position as the writer and secondly the sort of analytic tools I am offering the curriculum evaluator or researcher are economical in terms of data. They represent an approach to curricular proposals in which the bulk of time is spent doing analysis rather than collecting data. The tools are collected in two stages. In the remainder of this chapter I point out a large number of the rhetorical features of curriculum texts illustrating them by examples drawn from one text, that of *Moral Education in the Secondary School,*[7] and in the succeeding chapters I analyse these features more closely, thus suggesting methods for approaching aspects of curricular texts. Throughout the book, but especially in this chapter, it should be understood that the curricular texts from which examples and instances of rhetorical features are taken, are not being singled out for criticism. I use them not because I think they are *very* rhetorical nor because I think they are poorly researched, but because they are *convenient* illustrations of points *I* wish to make. This book is not a study of the curriculum texts which it cites. Rather it uses them selectively, without any regard to their overall structure or aims: it pillages them to make a collection of rhetorical devices. For a start then, this chapter seeks to point out, with next to no analysis, some possible areas for analysis — areas taken up in subsequent chapters.

## Some Guidelines

We start *not* with the beginnings of the research project, Moral Education nor with its premises, the basic ideas of the book, but with

Schools Council Project in Moral Education

Peter McPhail
J. R. Ungoed-Thomas, Hilary Chapman

# Moral education in the secondary school

the reader's beginning. And at least one place the buying, borrowing or
browsing reader may begin is with the cover and spine. The spine reads:

Moral education in the secondary school
McPhail, Ungoed-Thomas, Chapman

and the cover is as shown on page 26. The back cover contains a 'blurb'
— a flattering description of the book. Also available without going very
far are a notion of the 'length'[8] of the book and, in the case of my copy,
some indication of how others have classified it and where it has come
from. For just inside the front cover is a university library sticker and
number. That sticker tells us about the number of other readers, or at
least borrowers, (in this case twenty-nine). Other information includes
the price and the date of publication and the identity of the publishers.
However, these do not exhaust the things which the covers and their
insides can tell us. If we retreat a little in the shop or library so that we
can no longer discern the actual words on the spine or cover, we become aware of other features. The distance between blocks of words,
the type of lettering, the cover 'design', permit us to hold provisional
notions as to 'what sort of book this is'. These notions are not only
confined to classifications into 'academic' or 'thriller' categories, but
may be more precise. For instance, many readers will recognise an
HMSO, or Penguin, or Textbook publication from a distance. These sorts
of features may also suggest that the book is another in a known series,
i.e. similar to some others which we know about already. Consider then
both the graphical and verbal features of the cover as a *preface*.[9] They
tell us what we might find within and allow us to form provisional
assessments of the text. They do, however, more than this. First it is a
characteristic of excerpts of 'natural' language[10] that they are elliptical
or indexical[11]: that they do not, if you will, fully explain themselves.[12]
A short examination of any utterance or written sentence will show
that the hearer or reader *makes* sense of it by bringing to it his knowledge of who is saying/writing this, on what occasion and in what circumstances. Furthermore, to make sense of an utterance or sentence
the hearer or reader will have to know some of what was said or written
before.[13] Making sense is very much a contextual procedure involving
use of the immediate, local context of each utterance or remark and
more distant knowledge brought to the hearing or reading.[14] Sentences
may be grammatically complete but they do not make complete sense
on their own. Prefaces play a crucial role in helping readers make sense
of later pieces of text. They not only allow the reader to form a
provisional assessment of what the book is about, a reading to be

contrasted with some later 'fuller' reading of the text 'itself', they influence the later reading of the text itself. It is interesting that given this very powerful role possessed by such prefacial features as titles, author designations, covers, abstracts, etc. scientific and critical methodology seems little concerned with them.[15]

I do not want to suggest that these prefaces in any way 'control' later reading. The character of the assessments they permit is truly provisional and it is open to readers to find that the cover is, in this or that instance, misleading as to the real nature of the text. Even in that case, it should be noted that to find that one has been 'misled' itself influences further reading, making us more sceptical perhaps. At any event, the cover is worth some serious concern.

Many publishers also feel that covers matter and tell their academic authors so. They seem to have little formalised wisdom on how covers matter, but they are aware of their practical importance. Their common-place suggestions − that the use of this word might help sell the book; that the author might use this instead of that title; that covers imply readerships; that this design does not 'go with' that title; and that titles are important because of their position in the book − can be used to suggest five principles − principles which can be applied not only to titles but to rhetorical features of academic books in general.[16]

1. Ideas work through words and persuasive ideas work through words. One cannot apprehend 'bare notions'.[17, 18]

2. Writers have considerable freedom to choose which words they use. Scientific methodology only restricts *some* of that freedom.

3. Words can mean more than they say. They can suggest things.

4. Words can be combined and juxtaposed to produce effects through their influence in ways unknown to grammar (most obviously by conjunction in things like titles).

5. Spatial and chronological and narrative sequence are persuasive as well as 'logical' sequence. Where something 'comes' in the book is crucial.

These principles obviously relate to the earlier discussion of prefaces. Put together they suggest that writers may seek to persuade by so using words as to activate understandings that readers bring to the book; understandings about the topic of the book, about reading itself, etc.

Let us summarise these suggestions and the short discussion of prefaces simply by noting that writers have available to them ways of persuading readers which are not strongly controlled by scientific methodology and which derive from the character of reading. To read and make sense involves: bringing 'associations' to the text; involves attention to juxtaposition, contrast and combination; and orientation to spatial and chronological sequence. These are features of reading which are also potential features for persuasion. That, plus the author's freedom from tight methodological control, makes them practical as well as potential persuasive features. Let us now return to the materials.

## Achieving Authority Through Juxtaposition

Looking at the top of the front cover of 'Moral Education', notice first that we see three groups of words and a horizontal line:

Schools Council Project in Moral Education

---

Peter McPhail
J.R. Ungoed-Thomas, Hilary Chapman

Moral education in
the secondary school

We see three and not four groups of words despite McPhail being placed above the other authors, for we can see that McPhail could well be an author's name as could Ungoed-Thomas and Hilary Chapman and we see a line drawn between the first and second 'group' of words and the third group written in larger type. We also know the task of the reader is to see sense not to see graphics. If graphics help him find the three authors as with the line and the different type, so well and good. If not, as with the different alignment of McPhail from the other authors, then no matter. He can see the possible identity of the three surnames as authors as good enough for a provisional assessment. More, through noticing that the 'author' separated is 'first' (spatially) of the three he might see that the book was written by a principal and two subsidiary authors. None of this is announced. It is not announced that this group of words is one group, that another; that this is the title, that the author.

The reader has seen other books and comes prepared to find certain things on the cover in certain formats. In his effort to make sense of the whole (at least of the top part) of the cover, he starts to assign words into groups and pieces those to expected formats.

This book not only has the title and author declarations familiar on many covers; it has a third group of words:

Schools Council Project in Moral Education

What are we to do with that? What could it be? The words 'Moral Education' are in both the title and in this group; moreover, books often come out of projects. We might even see that either it could be 'The Schools Council Project in Moral Education in the Secondary School' abbreviated for 'design' purposes, or that the book title could be a sub-category of the research project, the research project having published or being about to publish one on primary schools as well. There is at least no problem, in our efforts to make sense of *all* the top half of the page, in seeing the book to be the book *of* the research. Given our knowledge of how such things are done and the page it is also possible to see McPhail and the other authors as members of the project with again possibly McPhail as the project leader. At any event the Schools Council does not lend its stamp to anything so there is some tie up between the authors and the project and the Council. Now I have deliberately said 'possibly' and expressed these associations casually. The reader/browser does not do a deep analysis of the cover: he does not treat it as a hypothesis. He *glances* at it. All I am suggesting is that there are a large number of ways in which that glance might suggest possibilities for making sense of the cover and, following Sacks,[19] I suggest that there is a rule in reading descriptions that possibilities should be realised: if you can read it that way then do so until you find discrepancy; most important, if you can see two or more items together, do so. Again, make sense where you can.

Now one other, rather different interest of the reader-browser, is not so much to see what sort of book it is but to evaluate it prospectively. Will it be any good? And one way of short-cutting that evaluation is to inspect the credentials of the authors. We can ask: 'Who are these people; McPhail, Ungoed-Thomas, Hilary Chapman anyway?' or further, 'Who are they to be writing a book on the curriculum?' Even further, 'Is there anything *on this* cover that might tell me who they are to be writing a book on this topic?' And there is, as I have shown, enough material on the cover to come up with a provisional answer to those questions. It is

further possible that they are members of a 'Project' and that they have
done things such projects do, i.e. 'research' and that as project members
they have been at it some time. Here then is a book which may well be
*authoritative,* which can be provisionally seen to be the result of sustained, 'research' work approved by a major relevant institution (even if
we do not know of the Schools Council its name ties it in with the
title). Thus the title accomplishes provisional authority.

In all this we must be careful. I am not suggesting that all browsers
read the cover like this. I am saying that some readers interested in the
topic will find a superfluity of clues on the cover which will lead them to
accredit the book with some authority. They do not have to reach a final
judgement. They can find later they were wrong. But the cover both
potentially persuades the reader that the book is good and persuades
that reader to buy, borrow, or read on. Throughout, this persuasive
process needs no evidence, no scientific logic and next to no grammar. It
is achieved by scattering words on a page in non-sentences but with
regard to sequence, juxtaposition, publishing and other reading and
social conventions, and word choice. Persuasive though these features
are, the methodology books, the criticism books, the evaluation books
have nothing to say about them. To a very considerable extent the
author is free to use such features as he will. This is not to suggest that
there is anything dishonest about the cover. I think, though I do not
know, that things are as they are suggested on the cover. The point is
that the methods for conveying this information are not the ones that
methodologists and evaluators examine. Academic texts, in this case
curriculum texts, work in practice through the organised use of words
and reading-writing conventions. A full method for examining or
evaluating them needs both to address the conventions and to look at
the organisation of words. For the organisation of words is not a literal,
nor a grammatical, nor 'logical' matter as we have seen.

**Organising Sequence: The Contents List**

Just inside the cover are more clues about the authority of the book.
Readers scrutinising these to establish, provisionally, the authority of
the authors will find that the book has been approved for acceptance
by a university library, has been borrowed by twenty-nine persons
entitled to use that library (with all that implies) and is published by a
well-known and reputable publisher. Once again such authority is both
provisional and casual. I am not suggesting the reader lingers over the

identity of the publisher, but not only does that identity tell the reader something positive about the book and its authors, what that identity is *not* is also important. The book is not by 'Camden Leninist Books'. It is not privately published. When we start to read the body of the text we are prepared to 'suspend disbelief', to treat the book both as 'a proper book on the Moral Curriculum which may well have something to say' written by people who may well 'know what they are talking about' and as academic comment rather than ideological pamphleteering. The author who can start off with his credentials thus provisionally established starts with a considerable advantage. Further, we can notice another principle in all this. The clues that point to authority or any other rhetorical feature of the book are not only mutually informing and reinforcing but superabundant. We fall over them everywhere. While it is true that readers read differently and many may not see each aspect of the cover and inside as *I* see it, these aspects are not concealed or exotic. It is difficult to get to the body of the text without acquiring some notion of its authority from one or two of these aspects, especially if one is a critic or evaluator and is interested in such matters.

And just as clues to authority are superabundant, clues to enable us to reach certain other assessments about the authors are massively absent. Curriculum innovators are, in conversation, quick to assure the listener that they do not know all the answers, that what looks like a 'project' is really only two or three under-resourced people in a prefab, that even these three members are not always in agreement, that research is not as solid as it seems. When these innovators write, they often employ the fashionable style of tenativeness; their projects are 'merely a start, towards something, obviously to be adjusted in practice by teachers', etc. Furthermore the ideas or materials may only be of interest or use to a few teachers and need to be developed by them. But covers, titles and the rest are not the places for modesty. Even when they explicitly state that they are 'working papers' or 'introductions', that does little to create in the reader an awareness of tenativeness, controversy, doubt, inefficiency, poor finance, etc. The solidity of the book and its implicit authority far outweigh any explicit humility, though explicit humility may be a useful ruse to fall back on in the face of subsequent criticism and may also seem polite and considerate to the reader. Thus one rhetorical feature we shall return to is not only the achievement of authority but the achievement of authority-with-modesty.

After the library identification and a repeat of the title we find the list of contents. See page 33.

## CONTENTS

Browsing academic readers may be observed in libraries and book shops looking for and reading contents lists (and indices) with attention. What they may well be doing is trying to form an idea both of what the book is about and what it 'covers'. I have already noted the freedom which authors have to choose their titles and certainly they have a similar freedom with the *words* they use in contents lists. Up to a point they can make a book appear to be about this rather than that and suitable for this rather than that readership. While physics cannot be turned into economics, research reports and theses can be 'disguised' as books, evergreens can be made to appear topical, 'theoretical' books can be transformed into 'practical' books and so on. Conference organisers will have noted the phenomenon whereby on a conference being pre-announced to be on topic X, all sorts of people who have never been interested in X manage to relate their work to it, sometimes by simple conjunction of the author's and conference's topics. Assessors of research grant applications with topically limited remits and appointment committees with specific jobs to offer have the same problem. For the fact is that academic work in the social sciences is not rigorously topic specific. What any piece of work is really 'about', what it implies, and what it should be classified under are not easy to ascertain. Librarians have enormous problems on account of this, as do readers trying to find books.

One consequence of this *topic licence* (and one *not*, I think applicable to *Moral Education*) is that it is open to the author to choose the standards by which his work is to be judged, for titles select not only readers but critics. The type and scope of scrutiny to which a book is subjected, the sort of question that is asked of it, depends on what it is seen to be, and to be about.

But not only can the author choose, within limits, how he is to identify his book and each chapter, but he can choose their length and order. McPhail and his associates were not forced by their research to organise their book into two parts, two appendices and eleven chapters. No logic *required* that the chapters be in the order they are, and of the duration that they are. On the other hand such matters may be extremely important in persuasion. Consider not only this text in which the authors and the blurb explicitly claim that the book is the result of the research, but any study that is perceived by the reader to be the product of work other than itself. The work which went on did so for months or years. It consisted of a myriad of activities, some short and some long, some linked methodically to others, some not. Some were productive, some a waste of time. After each, decisions were made to do something else; some of these decisions were *ad hoc,* some theoretical. Whatever else it may be, social science research is not entirely plannable or predictable.[20] More obviously, research has a chronological order — 'we did this then that' — and a 'logical' order — 'we did this because of that'. Less obviously it will not be clear *during* research whether some of the activities belong to the 'this' or 'that' categories. To be brief, much of the order of research is retrospectively constructed. What was hazy and muddled at the time, we can now see was a turning point and such and such was, though time consuming and also expensive, trivial.

Research reports are then accounts about past events made up backwards. They are accounts *about,* not *of,* past events. In the writing of them the author once again has licence. For his audience does not want a diary in which minutes are accounted for but an interpretation of the logical dynamic of the research. It also follows that different audiences want different interpretations for they have different interests. The financial sponsors of a curriculum project want a different report from the teachers who may read *Moral Education.* Thus if the book *Moral Education* is *about* the research, it is also *for* the reader. The decisions about chapter length, etc. and topical inclusion are not taken purely 'as a result of' research but are one way of interpreting the research in a specific context. The book is a tale of some past events, a tale consistent with the research but still a tale constructed for the occasion of its telling. Given this licence, this considerable licence to order, extract, omit, and connect pieces of the research in a number of ways and orders, the reader is essentially in the hands of the author and must trust him not to abuse this licence. But what is use and what abuse? Chapter length does suggest importance and suggest length of research; how intimately need these be connected? Is the neat allocation into chapters a fair representation of the ambivalence of research events? Does not the chapter organisation one to eleven suggest perhaps that this was the chronological order in which the research got done? Are the Parts One and Two not so ordered to suggest that Two is the product of One? Is 'Motivation and the morality of communication' an attractive way of grouping some thoughts, disparate in many other aspects, or the name of a time phase in the project or what?

Moreover the contents list works as a whole; it indicates a whole; it makes the book a whole with separate logically divided parts. The contents list and its implementation in later chapter organisation produces coherence. The book coheres because the book is made to cohere, not necessarily because the research coheres. And as numerous philosophers and literary critics will explain, coherence is not only

tied up with style, but with truth and plausibility. Addressing the
contents list is really an abbreviated and illustrative way of addressing
the order of the book, of grasping its topic, its sub-topics and their
relationship. Far from being dictated by research, the order of the
book, the conventions of chapter organisation, topical development,
citation, etc. offer the researcher a way of seeing and presenting a
version of his research both clearly and persuasively.

These comments do not cease to be relevant when we turn from
loose covers and fly leaves and look at the body of the text itself. For
although we are, with the latter, dealing with portions of text which
are (titles, page numberings, etc. excepted) in sentence format, the
principles we have listed earlier — principles of sequence, juxtaposition,
etc. — still apply. There is, however, one difference. Although critics
and evaluators take little interest in things like covers, they take considerable interest in the body of a book's text. This body is the part of
the book which, in the case of academic works, is supposed to be under
methodological control, and hence, which is to be evaluated or
criticised. If in my remarks about covers, I have been suggesting an
additional area for critics and evaluators to look at, in my remarks
about the body of the text I shall be suggesting a new way of looking
at some old and familiar issues.

**The Body of the Text: Licence to Start**

Part One, Chapter One of *Moral Education* starts as follows:

I. Why moral education?

The members of the Schools Council Moral Education Curriculum
Project believe that our principal adult responsibility is to help
boys and girls live well — live well in the sense that they learn to
care and choose. We believe this as a result of a four-year study
of secondary school pupils' needs. We are convinced that the fundamental human need is to get on with others, to love and be loved,
and that it is a prime responsibility of organised education to help
meet this need.

Paragraph Two announces the book's concerns to be the demonstration that 'our sons and daughters' rightly expect this moral education; the explanation of its processes; and the introduction of a
relevant school programme. The programme (Lifeline) employs

'everyday social learning situations to motivate the pupils, and is based
on the tenet that considerate behaviour results in social and psycho-
logical benefits to the actor.' The text continues:

> Few adults deny outright that we are responsible for the health,
> happiness and moral development of our children, but very many
> assume that these benefits will "happen along" without any special
> effort on their part. Perhaps they believe that the school has always,
> directly or indirectly, taken care of children's social and moral
> development and will continue to do so?

and it concludes by suggesting the need for a *conscious* policy of moral
education based on the organisation of contagious attitudes. In the
next paragraph it is claimed that children have expressed this 'need' to
the authors or adult researchers ('us').

> The Schools Council Report *Young School Leavers* showed that
> at least 70 per cent of fifteen-year-old boys and girls who leave school
> at that age expect the school to help them in two ways, first by
> increasing the understanding of what makes an action good or bad,
> and second by assisting them to find solutions to their interpersonal
> difficulties. They look to the school to help them carry out good
> courses of action, to support them when they do so and to be the
> kind of society which practices at all levels what it preaches about
> relationships. About 70 per cent is a particularly well supported
> figure. Philip May of Durham University in the research which he
> quotes in his book *Moral Education in the School* gives around 70
> per cent as the percentage of boys and girls in his enquiry who
> expected the school to be active in moral education.

The authors then point out that two of their own researches
produced support for this.

Focusing largely on the verbatim section of these first three pages of
*Moral Education,* but using some other extracts, I wish to extend the
list of rhetorical features. First and very superficially the sheer licence
of paragraph one should be stressed. The authors start the book how,
when and where *they* like. And they title the first chapter how they
like. They also title the chapter and select its first paragraph to fit each
other: 'Why Moral Education?' . . . 'Because the members of the Schools
Council', etc. And that first paragraph 'sets up' some reasonable next
things to do, in particular to extend the description of their 'four-year

study' and to explain why they 'believe' and 'are convinced'. They use
then their first paragraph to suggest what might be coming and to set
a tone. Readers know that early parts of books are routinely used to do
things like this and they treat them accordingly. They do not stop after
Paragraph One and bemoan the lack of evidence for this extravagant
creed. They wait for that evidence. They suspend their doubts. At this
stage all I wish to point out is that books consist of a large number of
places where things can be 'put'. They have chapter ones, later chapters,
acknowledgements, notes and appendices. Where statements get put in
part influences how they get read. It also influences what sort and how
much scrutiny is directed at them. But the structural 'effects' of these
statements may ramify for pages or chapters afterwards. How it starts
influences how it continues. Further, Paragraph One of *Moral
Education* seems a reasonable paragraph one. It is highly rhetorical in
its form with the repeated beliefs 'Project believe . . . We believe . . . We
are convinced', with its extreme measurement 'the fundamental human
need', with its matched words '*c*are and *c*hoose' and matched terms
'love and be loved' (and the semi-biblical connotations of these terms),
with its quasi-redundant definition of living well, its unnecessary
extension of getting on with others (love and be loved) and its sonorous
self-characterisation in the third person and at length 'The Members of
the Schools Council Moral Education Curriculum Project'. But first
paragraphs are one place (along with last paragraphs) where high
rhetoric may be admissible. Indeed it is not only admissible there but,
some believe, desirable. A *strong* start or finish are to be commended.

Impressed by its high tone we await a more logical argument and
some evidence in the paragraphs and pages to come. And these we *do*
receive. There is no doubt of that in the case of *Moral Education*. The
first and early paragraphs encourage us to expect certain arguments
and evidence and the later pages supply them. As we reach them we can
see how they answer and explain and extend earlier statements. What
we may not see is, that in encouraging us to expect certain arguments
and evidences, the rhetorical start may displace our own or any other
existing expectations. It enables the author to ask his own questions,
to define his own topics, to set up his own controversials. As well as
'working up' his own topic, this aspect of licence allows him to 'cut
out'[21] other questions, interests, controversials. If we remember that
this is not simply a matter of Paragraph One but that many books
adopt an *unfolding* style in which we are lead from conclusions *back* to
evidence over a series of chapters, then the structural effects of this
style are not only deep but wide. Two separate aspects need attention.

First, by stating the problem at the beginning we are encouraged to look at the evidence (when it is revealed) only or largely for its implications for the problem. In fact social science data are often ambivalent in their implications. Excluding very strongly controlled experiments, such research not only does not suggest one clear result, it does not suggest one clear question. It is multi-implicative, it casts light, if not precisely at least on *lots* of issues. It also *can* if it is allowed to, cast light on the relative merits of rival issues. If, for instance some data are given in a fairly raw form, they can be used to *attempt* to generate several questions. But once they are buried in a book, in, that is, another structure, they lose their openness. They are now only cited in service of the book-structure either in the sense that we only look at them for matters relevant to the argument of the book or worse in that frequently they are 'edited' for the book. Data are not to be understood then to be simply 'material acquired by conventionally accepted research procedures', they cease to be data if they are *displayed* in certain ways, if their structure is interfered with by the structure of the presenting medium, be it a seminar or a book. How data are presented in a book and *when* they are presented are crucial to this.

Secondly, the links between title and paragraphs, between paragraphs and paragraphs and between chapters and chapters are important. One paragraph may answer questions raised in another, extend the issues of another in a certain direction, summarise aspects of another and so on. The crucial aspect of all this is that paragraphs and chapters unfold in a *direction,* more precisely in some directions and *not* others. They are developmentally organised. At each point of development other possible developments are 'cut out'. Cumulatively the book narrows and details understandings so that rival understandings and interests, while always possible, become difficult for the reader to sustain. There are bits of the book which support them but the structure of the book does not. All this leads us to the question of the trust the reader can have in the author. Considerations of both size and readability dictate that research be 'arranged' for publication, that books have topical direction and that they be designed to be read. Anyway, there are no forms of communication, at least in natural language, that would not exhibit such characteristics as we have discussed. One lesson is obviously that these presentational features of books lose much of their capacity to fog and narrow issues when the reader is aware of them. Another is that the reader, aware now that the book is the creature of its author and neither the 'result' of research nor a neutral resource with which to set up and address different issues, short-cuts his problem by looking to the character of the author. Surely if the author is properly qualified, responsible, with good academic credentials and knows his subject he can be trusted to present a faithful version of his research if not a complete or accurate one? The problem with this short-cut is that often the only way to establish the credentials of the author is through examination of the text. Authors do, in fact, spend large amounts of text characterising themselves. Thus Paragraph One tells us (if we missed the cover clues and blurb) that the authors are accredited by a famous national body, have done four years research, etc., etc. If we want to use our assessment of the author to know how to read the book, we have to read the book to know how to assess the author and the picture of *him* which we get from *it,* is at least partly drawn by him.

### Ironic Contrast: Making 'News'

Passing on, we encounter yet another research presentation issue with the section 'Few Adults . . . so?' One matter that authors and publishers, indeed ordinary story-tellers have to attend to is novelty. For one dismissive response of readers and hearers to impeccably credentialled, evidenced arguments is 'What's new?' or 'So what?'

Authors are not usually content to let the fact that their book is 'news' be found out by the end. They take pains to announce or imply it at the beginning. The early lines of *Moral Education* set up an argument to which I and presumably the authors can see a possible reaction 'So what?' or 'What's new?'. And one sensible thing for them to do at the end of Paragraph Two is to squash this unfortunate reaction. They have argued for moral education. Even given their case it may be rejoined that such education exists already. So they must argue that their sort does not and cannot exist without a conscious effort, and that to help such an effort they have produced all these materials. Whether or not the authors fear that the reader who asks 'So what?' or 'What's new?' may in consequence abandon the book and the argument, or whether their rejoinder to it is merely there as a neat way of leading in to the following section need not concern us. For our purposes it is a splendid example of a popular rhetorical device — *ironic* contrast. Consider a simplified maxim of research lore:

Good Data + Good Argument = Good Conclusion

Practically minded researchers who want to attract funds, be published and not be unemployed have to supplement this with a concern for interest. If indeed they supplement it and not replace it with a concern for interest, with an effort to make the research appealing as well as right they may produce:

> Good Data + Good Argument + Contrast with Prevailing View,
> Popular Belief etc. = Interesting and Good Conclusion

Thus, as Wes Sharrock and I have suggested elsewhere,[22] social scientists love to show that the popular view is wrong, that things are not as they seem, that beneath the surface there are deep structures, that the mad are sane, that criminals are good and policeman bad, that existing policies are wrong, that past research was misleading, etc. And the point of all this as regards rhetoric is that while they often have evidence for their own conclusions they seldom offer any to show that people really do have the views which they wish to over-turn, contradict, etc. The *Moral Education* piece is a good example of this. If the authors have any evidence to support their statements about what 'very many' 'adults' assume, they do not declare it. But not only is the statement unsupported, it is a version of another popular rhetorical device, that of accrediting practical people with theoretical ideas (usually in order later to disprove the theoretical ideas).[23] The problem with so many questions which researchers pose to 'ordinary' people (or write as if they have posed) is that they allow the answerers 'Yes' and 'No', sometimes 'A lot' or 'A little', but rarely all four. People *do* have views about very particular issues as they arise and they do take into account details of circumstances. Their views which are tied to practical decisions may be very precise. They may have views about whether their elder son needs to learn X at this time or more likely should *have* been taught X. They are, of course, capable of generalising during conversations and on rare occasion doing so systematically. But quite often decisions, practical views and systematic or unsystematic generalisations are not tightly linked. To get through life as distinct from commentating upon it one needs a high regard for 'it depends', for the weighing of the details of this case, and most educational and social model theories do not last very well as *substitutes* for practical contextual reasoning. It is, then, first of all unclear whether the authors have *any* evidence for their attribution of beliefs to 'very many' 'adults'; secondly, notable that whatever the adults said (if they were asked) their words have been transformed into those of the authors with all that that transformation implies; thirdly, that whatever they did say was probably not offered as a candidate theory to be contrasted with the conclusions of research; fourthly, that it may have very uncertain connections with their actual views and behaviour in particular situations. The passage is also note-worthy for another device (indeed one I use myself) in the use of quota-tion marks to suggest that 'happen along' is a quote with no clear expla-nation as to who owns the quote but a convenient potential owner in the many adults mentioned five words away. It is one of many devices, another being the use of some specific social group's argot, which emphasises the author's access to the group if not his research of them. As we discussed earlier, one way to find that the argument is reasonable is to find that the author is reliable and knows what he is talking about. Demonstrations that the author is close to his subjects play a part in this.

Irony, through the use of a contrast with popular or current academic opinion, is a frequent component of curriculum packages. The risk is always there that those teachers who believe that there is nothing new under the sun might dismiss one's hard work without a second glance, and with some projects the publishing pressure to *be* novel or *display* novelty is enormous. Also in education new initiatives seem more marketable than developments. While it is true that *research* can be new in the revelatory or contrastive sense of the word, it is not often the case that it is so. Within sociology and education at least, there is not often enough replicability, not often enough reworking of other researchers' data for one study effectively to oppose another, so opposition has to be 'stylistically' generated. To this end, particularly, introductions are used to classify others' work in an extreme and con-trastive way, to set up opposites; oppositions being far preferred to continuations. In this way the book may become *about* the contrast with another position or just with the current state of teaching in X, rather than about the research.[24] What happens is that the *interesting* factor in the equation takes over the conclusion and misuses the research to justify itself.

### Borrowing Research: Citation

But research is not only done by curriculum innovators; it is borrowed. In Paragraph Three we find references to other people's research, in particular the work of Philip May. In this instance I do not think that the citation of May's work is at all crucial for the *Moral Education* authors' argument and I use it largely as an excuse to raise some wider issues about citation.

Education is a parasitic discipline. In particular it is parasitic on psychology, philosophy and sociology and its research is generally parasitic on methods established in the first and third of these (together perhaps with history). This means that like all academic disciplines it cites. Unlike many others it cites from 'outside' subjects. Education is also an applied discipline and curriculum innovation projects, for instance, may be so concerned with application, relevance, the opinions of teachers, the production of classroom materials and other matters, that they have little time for 'research' in the most rigorous sense. Both the applied and the parasitic status of education mean that use of other people's research assumes large and peculiar proportions. As a brief illustration, the Schools Council Health Education Project 5 – 13[25] is hung on three concepts, 'career', 'decision-making', and 'self-concept' all borrowed (at least in terms of original source) from disciplines external to education. The borrowing of these is no small matter for the project, and this large dependence of education in general on borrowed justifications (methods, knowledge, associations and concepts) raises several issues, which are highlighted in one borrowing technique, that of *citation.*

Citation is, seemingly, methodologically controlled. There are rules about how to do it and there is a check on its abuse. This check is the ability of the reader to go to source to see if the borrowed article is genuine. I suggest that the rules are woefully minimal, however, and that this is of crucial importance when arguments are highly dependant on citation, for example when a curriculum project bases itself on a state of wisdom or a set of concepts alleged to have been established in a foreign discipline.

Let us look at how readers use citations and differentiate several quite distinct usages. The same formula such as a number in the text or a name followed by a declaration of author, title, publisher, date and place of publication together perhaps with a few words of explanation is read as:

1. A (partial) *justification* of an argument in the citing text. It is evidence that others think likewise, or of others' research.

2. A *precision* of a point made in the citing text. The citer does not want to encumber his argument with details so he refers the detail-hungry reader to the bibliography or notes.

3. An *extension* of the topic in the text. 'If you like this and want to read more, look at . . .'

4. An *instance* of a rule or generalisation in the body of the citing text.

5. An *explanation* of how the author got to making his remarks in the citing text. This is one use of the barrage of citations employed by psychologists at the opening of articles. The barrage may also of course be a justification.

6. A *demonstration* that the author knows of a cited text which might be supposed by a reader to be connected with a point in his text.

7. An *example,* not, as in (4) above, of a point in the text, but of a field of work outside, a double citation in which the cited work invokes yet more.

These citation formulae also perform rhetorical functions:

8. They may show, as it were, the company the author keeps. They demonstrate that the author has access to certain resources. They also demonstrate that the author has access to a *number* of resources either by employing a lot of citations or by using them generatively as in (7) above. In any case they help in establishing the authority of the author.

It is worth adding that the establishment of authority is not only achieved by the author demonstrating *his* access, his 'friends'. For the effect of citation is to redefine the topic of a study. By suggesting the relevance (implicitly) of the cited studies the author refines his topic's boundaries. The particular form the topic takes in the end, whatever that might be, is usually such as to be closer to the author and further from the reader. The author has read the cited material. Usually the reader has not. At least the way the author puts it, the cited material is relevant. Thus whether or not we, the readers, thought we knew about 'Moral Education' before reading the McPhail book, the dual effect of reference to the author's own research and citation of others which we have not read, is to make us question whether we do in fact know as much as we thought, or as much as McPhail. In writing about a subject an author not only changes it then, he makes it *his own* and in so doing he moves it away from us. We no longer have control over it, access to it, knowledge of it in quite the same way for 'it' has changed. If we consider this together with what has already been said about authority, it can be seen that the authority of the author may be established through the way the author characterises himself in the book, as with the cover. It may be done through the way the author characterises his topic and his relation to it. Or it may be done through the way he detaches his reader from the topic by characterisations of the topic or the reader. For convenience the latter are called *distancing techniques.*

In addition to this, the use of citation, indeed the clear display of citation in easily detectable formats at the end of chapters, is another 'clue' that the book is 'academic' and to be read as such. The presence of citation formats, easily detectable by the browsing reader or borrower can be added to other cover features to see what 'sort of a book this is likely to be' and like those other cover features it not only arouses expectations but influences the way we read indexical or elliptical items in the body of the text.

All this points to an 'additional' aspect of citation: as well as referring us to the cited text, the citation may have these rhetorical features. But there are rhetorical aspects of citation which intrude more closely on the actual process of citation itself. First, just as the relationship of book to research is one of consistency rather than one of entailment: just as the book is a version, a 'tale' of the research so the citation is a version of the cited document. A small piece of the original document is removed and inserted in the citing text. We are just starting to appreciate how much any piece of a book, say *Moral Education,* is tied up by mutual influence, juxtaposition, etc. with other pieces in the same text, how a book coheres. This applies to the cited text as well. To remove a piece from source text to citing text is a radical act.[26] It transfers it from one rhetorical domain to another. The item will find itself on a new page, under a new heading, connected, compared, contrasted and juxta-posed with new items, in a new sequence, a new argument, with new givens, new conditions of trust, doing work for a new master and being read by a new reader.

In the transfer from page to page the piece *first* loses its equivocality, its restrictions, its uncertainty. Facts *in* texts are often hedged around by both reader and writer with qualifications. They are reasonably true, in these or those circumstances, for these or those purposes. They are true enough. The simple citation or process removes all this doubt and dirt and the fact comes through strong and pure:

> Philip May . . . gives around 70 per cent as the percentage of boys
> and girls in his enquiry who expected the school to be active in
> moral education.

The readers of the citation, unlike the readers of May's book, know
nothing but this. They have no reason for doubts, no 'ifs' and 'buts',
no circumstances, no possible worries about May's methods of research.

The second aspect of citation is that it obscures the organisational
context in which all facts are produced. Research does not often
produce open results, that is results which may be used indiscriminately
by anyone anywhere for anything. To use its results one has to be
aware of who produced them, in what circumstances and for which
clients. Simply, what will do in one circumstance, for one client, will
not do for another. Sometimes, unless one has a knowledge of the
producing organisation one cannot even understand its research, or at
least its intended implications. Often, for example, 'results' cited will
have been adequate to justify the original author's hypothesis and are
thus 'results'. They may well not be adequate to ground the conclusions
or suggestions of the citing text. There is no such thing as adequate
research. The issue is always 'adequate for what hypothesis, in what
circumstances given what research opposition, etc'. The *simple* citation
process sets aside such complications and in so doing nearly always
works to the benefit of the citing author.

Thirdly, the citing author has considerable licence in his choice of
references. The careful author will, as suggested in (6) above, wish
to show that he is *au fait* with works he might be expected to have
read. But above and beyond that there are millions of books in the
world and a lot of research going on. Out of all this the author needs
tens or at the most hundreds of references. In the social sciences
there is a widespread belief that every aspect of social life is interrelated with other aspects; that family, schooling, personality,
curriculum, economy, language, formal organisation, political factors,
etc., all affect each other. Currently there is a vogue for finding that
problems of, say, the curriculum occur in a wider 'situation' or
'context'. It may prove necessary, it is said, in order to see the problem
with Humanities education, to talk about the alienation of older
pupils,[27] or to cite a philosopher in support of one's suggestions.[28]
It might be necessary, in order to discuss the mass media and the
secondary school, to introduce questions of social class.[29] Or it might
be suitable in order to produce a new moral education, to base it on
interpersonal factors.[30] What the reader sees in working out a citation

is the connection between the cited remark or source and the argument in the citing text. What the citation procedure conveniently obscures is the sheer range from which the citation was chosen. The lack of replication and cumulation in the social sciences, the acceptance that what can be related is more important than what need be related, and the parasitic character of education combine to give the citing educationalist the key to an Aladdin's cave of justifications, examples, details, extensions and instances with which to ornament his argument.

These three factors are then combined with two others. The author often does not make explicit exactly which of the eight functions the citation has, though some citing sentences do start with 'for example' or explicitly say 'for further details see'. Often citations work in more than one of the ways. When the function is not explicit or is plural and confused the effect is to move the citation further from methodological control. It strengthens the writer's argument in one or more ways but since it works implicitly or confusedly, it is not available for the reader's scrutiny or counter-argument. Secondly and lastly, the control that the reader can, if he wishes, go to source to check the accuracy and suitability for citation in the context of the citing text's argument is not practical. The sheer range of documents which I have pointed out as open to the author to cite, and in the case of education the disciplinary variety make it unlikely that the reader will have access to them and more or less certain that he will not be competent in all their methodologies and organisations.

All the above combines to suggest that sometimes, I think often, the operation of citation in education texts is one of rhetoric and mystification rather than of method. Nor is such an operation confined to formal citations. If we adopt the terms 'borrowing' to refer to the invocation of someone else's work or judgement or statement, then there are a variety of ways of importing borrowed ideas, statements, results and judgements into a text. Less formal the citation is the use of examples or instances. Consider:

True one must not expect too much, too quickly, of say three-quarters of an hour's work per week in a secondary school, but improvement does take place, even if it is not always of a dramatic nature. *For example* one teacher in a very tough school reported that whereas at the beginning of a year's work using our material the children fought in their classroom by the end of that year they merely insulted each other.[31] (My italics)

Nor is this just a joke. For although the authors suggest this change probably owed much to the personality of the teacher they use the example as part illustration, part justification, four lines later: 'Nevertheless something useful happened and material provided one context within which it could happen'.[32]

With examples like these of 'real' events, not hypothetical examples, and of events reported by someone else than the author, we find the same problems as with citations. The example does powerful work for the author but we know so little of the original events which it relates that it can only help us to believe the author's argument not to scrutinise it. Perhaps, rather than say it relates some real events from outside the text, one ought to say that it tells a tale about them and in the telling replaces the structure of the events with the structure of the tale.

If examples are less formal borrowings than citations, it is possible to find less explicit borrowings than examples. First, examples are not always announced as such. They are not always introduced by the formula 'For example'. Secondly, one of the aspects of borrowing is the disavowal of responsibility. In citation, the author passes responsibility for the fact, result or comment cited to another author; in the sort of examples I have discussed the tale is only being 'repeated' by the author, it is not *his* tale. This disavowal for the cited item or example can be achieved by other means. Quotation marks enable an author to use a concept without endorsing it:

> If we look honestly at the notion that the young school leaver is uniquely in need of *'moral education'* we find that it is compounded of many elements, some of them exceedingly dubious. For example, being more *'intelligent'* may be a characteristic of some of those who stay on at school after fifteen, but being more intelligent does not necessarily mean that you are better able to find and apply solutions to interpersonal problems where the key is so often emotional.[33] (My italics)

And the reader will find many more examples in *my* own text. For it is worth repeating that there is nothing 'wrong' with such disavowals. If I wish to describe something as 'not being what people would commonly call wrong' it is a convenient shorthand to write 'there is nothing 'wrong' with . . . '. But it is a shorthand. It invokes something without justifying or detailing it. This, of course, *need* not matter. But if the invoked term, in this case the concept of intelligence, is one moment disavowed, introduced without justification or detail and the next moment used to further the argument of the author, it does matter. If the authors are members of the fashionable school which does not believe in the use of the concept of intelligence and wish to indicate this by putting quotation marks round it, all well and good. But it is less well and good, though not I think very bad, to use the 'useless' concept two lines later for the advancement of their argument.

We cannot know on what grounds the authors disassociate themselves from the concept of intelligence. That is the first problem with this borrowing practice. And we cannot know exactly what concept they disassociate themselves from and who they think does espouse it. That is the second problem. Both these become *problems* when we want to scrutinise their statement about intelligence and interpersonal problems two or three lines later. For that statement sets up a folk-lore contrast between the intellectual on the one hand and the emotional on the other. It offers no evidence. It does not have to, for it works like a *maxim*.[34] It is, or appears to be, self-evident. The readers all know that intelligent people can get themselves in dreadful emotional messes. Intelligence and emotions are just not the same thing.

It seems to me that the authors want to have their cake and eat it. They wish to trade off the folk-lore differentiation of intelligence and emotion while disavowing the concept of intelligence. I say 'seems' for I am uncertain. And uncertainty is the dominant aspect of borrowing. Ideas, terms, results, judgements, etc. can be borrowed in a large number of ways, some very formal, some less so. Indeed, one highly informal technique is to use, without quotation marks, the argot of a group of people one is talking about; another derives from the associations with certain people outside the text that certain words have. And in consequence the reader who tries to go through a text asking of each fact or term the question 'Is the author making himself responsible for this, is it *his*?' will find he is often uncertain. Equivocation and ambivalence are old argumentative techniques. But they do not just apply to topics. One can be equivocal about *what* one is saying and about whether one is really saying it oneself.

## Caution

Students learning the art of academic expression learn this equivocality
as part of their education. They learn to say 'it seems', 'there is some
evidence for', 'on the one hand', 'while X . . . yet Y'; they learn to use
doses of conditionals and subjunctives 'we would argue'; they learn to use
double negatives. They learn to *write-so-as-to-appear-cautious,* sometimes
even humble. This style can have the advantage of reflecting the
difficulties of reaching certain and sure conclusions in education.
Consider:

> 'Follow up questioning . . . *suggested* that at least 70 per cent of
> adolescent boys . . .'[35]
>
> *We cannot afford to ignore* such evidence'[36]
>
> 'This research also *showed* that . . . were not the prerogative of any
> social class.'[37]
>
> *'There was certainly no indication that we can afford to regard*
> early school leavers as a special class'[38]

(Italics in all the above are mine)

And on the same two pages from which these are taken, we find:

> True . . . but . . . not always . . . some of them . . . may . . . some . . .
> does not necessarily mean . . . so often . . . Frequently . . . such as . . .
> may . . . The need is not specific to . . . may be subconsciously . . .
> We see in . . . warnings that there is . . . far too much . . . It is not
> that . . . Perhaps . . . We should pay attention . . . seldom . . . In one
> way . . . we tend . . . Furthermore, we may.[39]

It is important to stress that the book *Moral Education* is probably
less tentative than most curriculum proposals. The authors go out of
their way to stress their commitment and frequently use the expression
'we believe'. They also make a lot of statements without qualification.
However, the expressions we have noted above as indicative of caution/
equivocation are only the most literal signs of it. Caution/equivocation
need not be announced. It can shine through the associations of individual words in context, through what have been called tropes: it can be
neatly, pervasively communicated by a series of finely balanced clauses
and colons, what neo-classical rhetoricians call figures or schemes: it can
be appended in notes, appendices and conclusions which retreat on

statements in the text; it can be prefaced in introductions and titles which warn that this study is only a 'contribution', an 'initial investigation', that it is 'towards . . .'!

Once again we can find in all this some by now familiar characteristics. First, the very procedure which is 'meant' to be 'scientific' offers possibilities for rhetoric, for persuasion through style. The persuasive devices I have been discussing come, not through abandoning the features of academic writing, but through using them both in an academic and in a persuasive way. Secondly, their effect is cumulative. Maybe the reader could sort out exactly what the author was claiming and how far *he* was claiming it, after closely examining one of the examples above. But they are one to ten words and the book is 60,000 to 80,000. Not only does this leave thousands of equivocations to be 'sorted out' but each equivocation influences others. They all influence the reader's understanding of the book and his picture of the author. For the interest of the reader is primarily at book and author level. His job is to make sense of the whole thing.

Thirdly, the fact that equivocation/caution can be implied as well as explicitly announced should alert us to the (theoretical) possibility that a text may announce itself to be cautious with plenty of 'tends', 'tentatives' and 'towards' but still manage to convey the impression that the author is certain, authoritative, etc. We return to these, as to many of the other matters raised, in more detail in later chapters.

### Lists and Levels

If equivocation obscures, lists clarify. And a familiar technique in face-to-face teaching and in textual explanation is to use a list. Lists are popular with both hearer-learners and reader-students because they abstract 'points' from prose and offer them in a concise, notable, numerically organised way. But once again it is in good academic practice that rhetoric can flourish. Consider the following list from *Moral Education* (page 30);

> The first step in following up the clues about personal education which came from our preliminary enquiry was obviously to set up a systematic large scale survey with adolescent boys and girls. The purpose of such a survey and any subsequent experimental work would be:
> 1.   to identify pupils' areas of concern – the problem areas in which they ask for help.

2. to use the evidence from 1 to prepare a preliminary definition or description of 'moral education'.
3. to use the evidence about motivation from the enquiry to help develop M.E. materials and techniques; the use of which would not only facilitate moral decision taking but also, and more important, motivate boys and girls actually to treat people 'better'.
4. to construct an M.E. programme which would cover all the principal areas of adolescent difficulty by using their 'situations' as the basis of materials.
5. to serve as an initial model for those wishing to develop M.E. programmes or supplementary programmes in other places at other times.

It was clear that such a survey would have to be concerned with the process of adolescent social and moral learning so that the natural learning process could be used in the Project's programme.

ADOLESCENT MORAL AND SOCIAL PROBLEMS

Our first question might be: 'What is this a list of?' For although the authors introduce it as a list of 'the purpose of the survey', its placement in the book, especially above the sub-heading 'Adolescent Moral and Social Problems', plus the resemblance of some of the items to the titles of later chapters (see contents list given earlier) suggests that it is an announcement of where the book is going to go and why. Specifically, Item 1 on the list can be read as referring to the sub-heading below, or indeed the whole of Chapter Two 'Identifying Adolescent Needs'. Item 3 ties to Chapter Four on motivation, and Item 4 to the whole of Part Two, Chapters Five to Eleven, on programmes. The individual items on the list, for example, the interest in 'situations' and 'treating people better' are argued for individually elsewhere. What the list does is to clarify the *organisation* of these items in the book, suggest some logical links between them and give a measure of their respective importance.

First, the list has numbers and the items with higher numbers are to be dealt with later in the book. Secondly, the later items are seen to be in some way the results or consequences of earlier items. Thirdly the effect of giving various issues slots in various items is such as to suggest amounts of importance. The authors could, for example, have used sub-categories. In fact they could have produced a list with twenty or with two items. Without having the relations between the items

announced to us explicitly we can see that you would do 4 after 1,
2 and 3. We can also see that the list makes sense. It is a fair enough way
to organise one's work.

Earlier I have suggested that much education research is rather
messy. Two questions that the research manuals are not very good at
helping researchers with are what to do when, and how much of each
bit to do. They can of course advise that pilots come before surveys,
that instruments come before experiments, that hypotheses come
before testings. But the more elaborate questions of how to get into a
loosely defined area, how many things to take into account, how much
time and how many pages to spend on each of them — these questions
researchers have to sort out for themselves, bearing in mind worthy
considerations such as aspects suggested by other studies and the state
of data availability and the less worthy considerations of their own
backgrounds, competencies, incompetencies, interests, ideologies, job
prospects, the financing of their project, the interests of their sponsors,
etc. The *direction, sequential organisation and balance* of a research
project are practical matters. Many of these are not decided in advance
or if they are, they may well be subsequently altered. Gradually, from
hindsight, the mass of data and ideas can be sorted into an orderly tale
of events, even a tale with a moral. Lists such as the one above are one
way of doing this job. Their rhetorical character lies essentially in that
they give, construct and assemble order rather than reflect it. Of course,
as I said in the discussion of contents lists, they must reasonably consist
with the parts of the research, but in the way the parts are fitted together it is the list which leads, not follows. There is an extent to which
they are arbitrary. The author can decide that he is going to have so
many parts to his book and put them together in such and such a
fashion. In its potential for confusing orders of logic, chronology, style
and intention, and in its ability to shake off the unresolved, the messy
issues and emerge with its items clean and clear, the list is deeply
rhetorical. Quite simply to place one item under another and allocate to
it a number one higher than the previous item, neither explains nor
justifies though it may well summarise the relation between the two
items. Once again we find this tension between a device which may well
have good presentational uses and be deeply rhetorical. Whether the
authors of *Moral Education* wish to use their list as one or the other is
not here the issue. In the introduction to the list the authors' use
of tenses and moods 'the first step . . . was to set up . . . survey . . . the
purpose . . . would be:' is such as to suggest that the list *was* set up as a
list of objectives prior to the research and this may well be so. As stated

earlier, I have no privileged knowledge about the research behind the texts. The point of the above remarks is not to suggest that the authors of *Moral Education* did or did not write lists at this or that moment, but to stress that readers of their or any curriculum text based on research do not *know* what happened and cannot easily separate out the different orders.

Lists like this are a sort of plan. There are other sorts of lists. Consider this list from *Moral Education,* page 10. It has no numbers and it is not set out like the other one:

> Many factors, including the decline in Christian belief, improved world communications, mobility of labour, immigration, the ideological nature of contemporary international struggles, increasing interest among the young in eastern religions and a problem of identity brought to crisis point by the rapid development of the mass society have highlighted the variety of standards and mores in interpersonal behaviour now recognised in the, until recently, insular United Kingdom.

An important aspect of a list such as this is its homogeneity. Although the items are topically very different, there is something about them which makes them a list of *like* things. Nor is this likeness merely their asserted nature as the common condition of adolescents. For example, adolescent David may have enormous problems with his father's grumpiness caused by toothache. That would not fit well on the list. Of course the list problems are all big, general, even societal problems. David's is particular. Furthermore the items have another common factor. They can all be linked to a problem *general* for adolescents, the need to choose between cultural varieties. This is the point the authors wish to make, for it will then add to the justification for their programme which locates moral education in choosing in social situations. Once again the rhetoric is in the order. A moment's thought will show that the list did not just happen. The list is not the unequivocal result of the authors pondering the problems and trends of the West. If they had pondered these, they would have got an eclectic list. No, the list is put together to produce the point about variety and choice. The point comes first but is put in the book second. This is not to say that the authors had no reasons for thinking that variety and choice were problems for adolescents but they certainly were not these. In reality perhaps the reasons were more complicated. The authors perhaps decided that variety and choice were more important problems *than some others* which they discarded. These others they do not discuss. They would be irrelevant for the book. The book should be readable. It should entice the reader along. This is exactly what this section does. It is a piece of writing which offers a list and resolves the puzzle in it with a common factor which is matched neatly to an educational solution. The formula is: find a problem solution pair such as cultural variety-choice. There will be no need to justify it for it will be in the maxim format. Find pointers to the first pair part, arrange them in a list so that it can be produced out of them, then follow with the second. It is good writing but notice how the style affects the plausibility. Again the simple point: books are books; logic is logic; research practice is research practice. If you try and do your logic on practical research matters they will divert it: if you argue or present research in books they will affect the argument and research presentation.

## Practicality

It has already been suggested that curriculum research is often applied research. It is applied at least in that many projects are producing ideas, programmes, materials, perspectives or reports for consumption by practitioners. Authors generally spend some time trying to make this point. The title of *Moral Education* suggests that it might be of interest to secondary teachers. The Schools Council designation reinforces this. The publishers are, naturally, convinced of it. On the back cover they have:

> Moral Education . . . will be of interest to all concerned with the education and development of adolescents.

The contents list refers to actual teaching materials and the first page of the body of the text announces the authors' concern to introduce 'a secondary school programme'.

Throughout the book the reader finds pointers that the book both reports on a research project and that the research is the basis of an actual programme for use in schools. This notion that the research is for practitioners, is to result in a programme, is 'relevant', etc. is not a side issue. One might even put it on a par with that of research reliability. It is of the utmost importance that the book be both sound and reliable and useful and practical.

However much practicality, relevance and being 'applied' are approved as virtues, even crucial virtues in curriculum texts, there seems to have been surprisingly little thought given to exactly what they consist of. Rather notions such as these seem to be used as headings under which various different features are collected. A practical curriculum proposal may be thought to be one which has (a) *prose features,* in that it is written in a style which teachers will find reasonable and readable. It is written with the teacher as reader in mind. The authors will eschew the use of the 'jargon' of their disciplines and research. They will avoid excessive use of abstract nouns not common in daily talk. There will be lots of examples. There will be devices (such as lists) to help the reader 'understand', rather than devices (such as long arguments with many subordinate clauses as various qualifications of the point made in the main clause) which are difficult to follow.

Practicality may also be thought to include: (b) *design features* in that the book will be titled with teacher-purchasers/borrowers in mind. Further features such as contents lists, chapter headings, formats, cover designs, length, and price may be similarly adjusted to the publishers' and authors' views of the teacher-reader/borrower; and (c) *organisation features* for it will not only be titled to be 'about' teacher interests but will be organised so that the teacher can pursue his interests in it. It is permissible to place the research account in the early chapters but it must be made clear in and before those early chapters that the research was done and is being recounted to lead up to the programme for schools. If the teacher is expected to plough through all these researches and psychology and philosophy he must be reassured that there is a pay-off. So on page 3 of *Moral Education* (the first page of the body of the text) we find:

> Our book is concerned first to demonstrate that our sons and daughters expect to be educated in living well and are right to do so; second to show how they learn socially and morally, third and *most extensively,* to introduce a secondary school programme . . .

The book is not to be an account of the research to which is appended the afterthought that there might be 'some implications for teachers here'. It is organised around the production of a 'practical' programme. This organisation affects the directional structure of the book, what it includes of the research and from elsewhere and how these things are put together and built up in a sequence. It also affects what is left out. Among the piles of researches and the readings, decisions, and musings of the authors there will be a lot that must be left out of this book.

There will be a lot more of which even the authors are not aware, implications they have not seen because they are looking at their materials
from certain angles.

'Practical' is also used to suggest (d) *topical features.* A good applied
book will also seek to incorporate some of the world of its reader into
its text. It will talk of things with which the reader is familiar, in this
case of timetables, of answers, of age groups, of the connections with
the existing subjects, etc. This may involve actually using the professional language of the teacher in particular in referring to aspects of
the school.

> The pupils involved in using the *Lifeline* programme would, in our
> imaginary school, be Band B (the lower ability band) from the first
> to the fifth year (that is from eleven-plus to fifteen-plus). We have
> chosen the lower ability band, not because we believe in any way
> that pupils who do not find themselves in the highest forms need
> any more moral education than those who do; nor because the
> programme has proved in trial to be any less successful with pupils
> in higher classes. It is for the regrettable but practical reason that,
> while O-level continues to exist, exam orientated attitudes, rigid
> syllabuses, and a sense of anxious haste predominate in classes
> which contain pupils who have proved successful in coping with
> the school system. Such a situation can militate against time being
> spent on encouraging a considerate style of life among academically
> successful pupils.

It often involves taking the 'lots of examples' referred to in (a) above
from relevant domains.

*Level structure* (e) is frequently involved in the appearance of
practicality. The incorporation of the reader's world affects the level
at which matters are categorised. It is a commonplace observation,
particularly in sociology, that aspects of a society can be formulated
at different levels. This shows itself most clearly with problems. For
example: Simon's problems with his maths can be seen perhaps as an
issue of Simon's dislike for his maths, an issue of personal preference,
by Simon's parents. He does not do well because he has 'never liked
maths'. Teachers may see Simon's problems in teaching categories as
ones of motivation, application, abstraction. Pastoral Counsellors are
interested in the possible relations of Simon's academic with his other
problems. For others, Simon's difficulties are typical of those
encountered by many children due to the shortage of good maths

teachers. For yet others, the fact that Simon's school is in an urban depressed area is crucial. For others it is shortage of equipment caused by government cutbacks. The interrelatedness of social factors which I have referred to above encourages a disposition to see problems as possibly connected with personal, moral, administrative, political, local-social, national-social factors. And those factors are at different levels — personal, familial, school, local, national, etc. There is a corresponding disposition to see solutions as possible at different levels.

When a book is written for a particular professional group such as teachers, that group solves problems at some levels rather than others. A 'practical' curriculum book not only is readable by teachers but talks of solutions which could be operated at the level at which teachers work. A book which found the solutions to moral education problems in the increase of government expenditure or the overturning of capitalism might be of interest to some teachers but it would not be a 'practical book'.

Since solutions are required at teacher level, and since solutions should be relevant to the problems which they are to solve, it is only reasonable that authors should employ the considerable licence available in grading problems to characterise the problems in such a way as to show aspects of them which teachers can address. It is not that curriculum innovators deny other aspects of problems. In the Humanities project the authors admit:

> There are some situations in which it seems unlikely that schools can readily succeed. In those urban areas characterised by physical and cultural dereliction, where housing is bad and 'problem families' abound, there is probably no purely educational remedy. Only social reform on a broad scale can strike at the roots of the problem, and the best chance of amelioration through education will be where educational development and community development go hand in hand.[40]

But there is no point in pursuing such aspects, for although they are important they are not important here, in this case, for Humanities teachers reading an introduction to a curriculum project. So the authors continue:

> There is another style of alienation, however, which is much more widespread and much more susceptible of educational solution . . .[41]

and they go on to show what such problems are and how curriculum research can help. What authors are doing with such problems is not only finding aspects which might be addressed at teacher level but characterising problems so that they can be addressed at teacher level. For so often the same indicator such as exam failure, truancy figures, or the ratio of black to white children can be used to conceptualise problems at different levels. The task of the authors of the practical curriculum text is to work up their topic so that there is plenty for teachers to do.

In addition to these aspects of practicality, (a) to (e), there are (at least) two others: (f) some curriculum projects are concerned that teachers should *like* their products; (g) others are concerned that teachers should *use* their products. A curriculum package is practical if the people for whom it was written approve of it and/or if they use it in large numbers. Of course one can assess curriculum packages in more ways than this. One can *evaluate* them. But the judgement that a text is practical does not go as far as evaluation. It is concerned usually with the fact that it can be read, understood and put into action rather than with the consequences of such action.

I wish to suggest that these common understandings[42] of practicality are hopelessly muddled. First, a considerable number of them are not about the practicality of a curriculum text but are about the ease with which it can be read. A curriculum text which does not pay attention to the aspects of prose and design noted above will be impractical[43] because the people capable of putting it into practice will not be able to read or understand it. A curriculum text which does not pay attention to the features of design, organisation, topic and level will be impractical because the people capable of putting it into practice will not wish to read (or at least continue to read) it. These features are then important and pleasant features of practical texts but they are not sufficient. An author can produce a text which is styled, designed, organised, topical-ised and stratified for teachers and it may still be wildly impractical. Further, and this takes us into the realms of heresy, he can produce a text which teachers like and it may still be impractical. Lastly, and I can feel the faggots burning at my feet, he can produce a text which teachers *say* they use or which he *sees* them using, and it may still be impractical. How can these things be?

First, it must be accepted that academic authors do not have a monopoly on theorising or whatever the opposite of practical talk is. Teachers also theorise. It is possible for a teacher to like a curriculum text, to imbibe and accept its ideas, to retitle his lessons in line with it, to intend before the lesson to teach in accordance with such ideas, to look back afterwards and see that he did so, and still not *actually* do so. It is possible for curriculum evaluation and dissemination officers to watch a class and see it as an example of their curriculum package and for it not to be so. The problem is at least simple to diagnose. It is hopeless to say that a practical text is one which can be used if we do not establish what 'using a text' is. Clearly a text being 'in use' does not just mean that a lesson is titled in accordance with it or that some papers or kits from the text are introduced into the lesson. Curriculum Innovators are well aware of this issue and some are most annoyed when their materials are used/abused and their perspectives discarded.[44] But what does a perspective look like in use? Do we find it to be in use merely because disseminators 'see' it and teachers feel they have used it?

If all this seems terribly complicated, I would simply appeal to the widespread knowledge that just because someone thinks he is doing something different, it need not look any different to the observer.

There is a further issue. Presumably it is logically possible to have a curriculum text which is practical but for all sorts of extraneous reasons not practised. Practical refers to a feature of the text not a feature of the class.

To get at a reasonable notion of practical we have to ask 'Practical for what?' And I think that in common parlance when we refer to a book as practical, we certainly mean practical for the user-reader to read; we sometimes mean practical for the user-reader to say he likes or uses; and we often mean *practical for the context of use.* The actions suggested in the text must be doable by some actual persons to or with some other actual persons in actual circumstances. A practical text will spell out what such persons and circumstances will look like. Put differently, a practical curriculum text will contain as a minimum a workable model of the teachers, the pupils and the classroom.[45] If it does not contain these, then it is not really a practical curriculum proposal at all but a (possibly extremely practical) teacher-education device. If it does not contain these models or if it contains them but they are, like so many social science models, unarticulated dolls incapable of performing anything like a social action in context, incapable of taking a register even, this omission may well prevent it in certain circumstances being a practical curriculum programme. More interesting from the point of view of this study, it certainly will *not* prevent it using the rhetoric of practicality. It may well *look* very practical indeed.

A relevant question then to ask about an allegedly practical text is whether it is really practical. To answer that involves looking at the context in which the text is to be incarnated, then studying the text to see how it characterised the components of that context and inspecting the relationship between the two. This I do in chapter six. If we find that the book is not practical in this sense but that it appears to be 'a practical book' when read, then we might well look to see not whether it *is* practical but what rhetorical features are involved in *passing*[46] as a practical text.

Lastly, not only is there a rhetoric of practicality which helps the book pass as practical. This very rhetoric contributes to the reader's general characterisation of the book. And the effect of his acceptance of it, of his willingness to 'read this as a practical book' is to set aside other ways of reading it. Most obviously there is a possibility that a book which reports research will be read as a research book and judged by research standards. It will be expected to have, perhaps, long bibliographies, to exhibit 'scientific methodology' in detail, to argue in a very careful and heavily qualified way, to produce lots of evidence. But once the reader can see that, although based on sound research, the book is a practical book, then such standards, while not dropped, can be relaxed, for the prose style, book design, organisation, etc. of a practical book are not completely compatible with those of a research report as can be seen by inspecting the aspects listed under sub-headings (a) to (e).

The rhetoric of practicality is then doubly rhetorical. It helps persuade the reader that such and such is a good book with practical suggestions and it cuts out criticisms that might be used if the book were not 'practical'. Cynics might suggest it was triply rhetorical for it is less threatening to the practical than a genuinely practical book.


## Summary

Books exhibit certain features which I have been loosely grouping together under the heading 'rhetorical'. To say that a book has these rhetorical features is not to say that it is a bad book, for these features spring unavoidably from the concerns of the parties to the book, the authors, the publishers and the readers, and from certain features of natural language. In particular they are the products of the way that words mutually reveal and re-reveal each other, of the layers of meaning and association that words have in context, of the power of order and sequence. The authors have considerable freedom over such matters.

The fact that a book is academic means that the author has little less licence than a writer of fiction when it comes to these matters, for much residual scientific methodology does not address them, at least in education. These features not only occur in the body of a text but on its covers, its flyleaves, its contents list and its titles and chapter headings. They are pervasive. While they are only one set of features of a book, in this case a curriculum text, they influence the general nature of the book. The reader who would be truly critical of the text must take into account that, while it may be a research report or a curriculum programme or an argument about moral education, it is a report, programme or argument in textual form, in book form, in 'practical' book form.

To help such a discerning reader take them into account this long chapter has used and abused *Moral Education* to suggest some possible areas for investigation and analysis, and some techniques and orientations for that analysis. It cannot be too strongly stated first that this chapter is not a criticism of *Moral Education.* How could it be? It is not even a study of it. It merely uses it as an illustration of some points and as a prompt to what is little more than speculation on other points. The business of the chapter is neither description nor criticism but, I hope, the production of hunches — an imaginative bric-à-brac to be tried out on further material.

Imaginative[47] bric-à-brac does not fit very well into those diagrams[48] with boxes and arrows so beloved by systematisers in the 'applied' social sciences. It does not sit happily in a flow chart or algorithm. It would be an exercise in the crudest of rhetoric were I to try and fit it into a summary scheme or system. However imaginative, bric-à-brac, like the other sort, can be displayed rather than tossed in a pile so here is some sort of check list of the orientations of this chapter.

The reader who wishes to incorporate rhetorical features into his reading, criticism or judgement of a book should look seriously, not only at the 'ideas' in the book, but at the text, at the words. There are components of the text which can be readily discerned which he should address. They do not have to be hunted for. They can be detected for the most part by their spatial organisation. Some are:

1. Title on the cover
2. Authorial indication on the cover
3. Illustrations, etc. on the cover
4. Other words on the cover
5. As above on the spine and

6. Back cover especially the 'blurb'
7. Size of book
8. Shape of book
9. Library stickers
10. Price
11. Date
12. Contents list
13. Spatial organisation of lettering
14. Page numbers
15. Chapter size
16. Chapter order
17. Citations
18. Quotation marks
19. Lists
20. Appendices.

These are added to the body of the text which can be seen as words juxtaposed and organised into lines. The aim of the rhetorical analysis is to see what part the organisation of those components of covers, fly-leaves, lines, etc. play in the eventual credibility of the text. To do this it might be helpful to think of two stages in between the components and the conclusion of textual credibility. First there are a number of 'interim' conclusions which may support the eventual conclusion of text credibility such as:

1. A conclusion that the book is this or that kind of a book, in this case a 'practical curriculum book', and is thus to be judged as such and found suitable. The book is a good example of its kind. Notice that the book can characterise itself in the text. Call this the achievement of *Relevance.*
2. A conclusion that the text is authoratitive and that the authors know what they are talking about. Call this the achievement of *Authority.*
3. A conclusion that the book is 'the result of' the authors' research, or the result of the authors' use of others' research. Call this the achievement of *Factuality.*
4. A conclusion that what the authors have to say and offer is new. Call this the achievement of *Novelty.*

The problem can now be put 'How are the *components* of the text, the lines, the titles, the covers, etc. so organised to produce or support the achievement of relevance, authority, rigour and novelty?' In this chapter we have seen some of the answers to that question. A number of devices are used, most of which are based on the principles loosely listed towards the start of the chapter, the principles which I shall now call:

1. Incarnation. Ideas can only be got hold of through words and when these words are organised in ordinary language prose in a book they are characterised by
2. Indexicality.[49] Individually they mean nothing. We have to take their surrounding words and our understanding of 'what sort of book this is' *to them* in order to *make sense* of them. If we use each part of the book in order to make sense of the other, we also use the other to make sense of each. Our sense making is characterised by
3. Reflexivity.[50] We do not make sense only of line one then, using it, line two, but reinterpret line one retrospectively using our understanding of line two. Our work is to make sense cumulatively of the whole thing forming, destroying and refining our understanding.
4. Juxtaposition, Narrative and Sequential Order are powerful guides as to how to use each to see other and put *together* a reading of the text as distinct from a reading of a line.

But sequence and juxtaposition are very much creatures of the author. He can choose various forms of juxtaposition and sequence which support the reading he would like us to make, a reading which may lead to the achievement of authority, rigour, novelty and relevance. We do not have to read the text as he wishes but there are plenty of indications to encourage us to do so.

Within wide limits the author can set his own stage. He can set up contrasts, introduce new developments, shut off old ones, dictate order, decide spatial allocation, set the book's and argument's direction, make other direction difficult to envisage, provide evidence for his argument, not provide consistent evidence for the construction of rival argument, intertwine data and argument in the same chapter, the same paragraph, distance the reader from the topic by careful 're'-construction of the topic, collect himself in impressive company, decide and declare what sort of book he has written and thus control criticism, intermingle, logical, stylistic, book, and research order, disavow the statements he himself inserts in fine degrees and reach firm conclusions through cautious and equivocal arguments, at least firm enough to constitute programmatic offers.

If the reader is still sceptical let him try a little test. Let him take a curriculum proposal text and summarise it. He will have little difficulty for its implications will be clear (if not always practical). Then let him go through the text that 'supports' these implications, trying to write down exactly what is being argued by whom and how. Here he will have far more difficulty. Let him then judge whether the text supports the conclusion in a logical-scientific way. It will be surprising if he does not find that the only way of deriving the implications from the text is by reading the text rhetorically. Indeed it is doubtful whether he will even be able to continue reading it unless he takes note of the factors I have outlined.

Two footnotes: first, the rhetorical nature of such natural language academic texts as curriculum books does not mean that they are *just* words, that they have no evidence, no method and no logic. It means that their 'scientific' character is mediated through both natural language and the social organisation of books, publishing, buying, reading, etc. A notion of curriculum books which represented them as purely social or 'literary' would be as inappropriate to them as one which treats them as ideas or research. For a balanced view we must return to the point at which we began — the reader. A text is how the reader reads it and he reads a curriculum text for ideas through words. So must we.

Secondly, I have deliberately avoided in this chapter showing the number of 'ornaments' in the text, the number of devices we tend to associate more with poetry or formal speeches. Lest anyone think the figures and tropes; the conquestios or appeals to the emotions, the amplificatios or emphases in the conclusion, the interrogatios or questions which need no answer, the rogations or self-answered questions, the isocolons or phrases of equal length, the parisons or formally matched cola and the other paraphernalia of semi and classical rhetoric[51] are not to be found in academic texts, I finish this chapter with quotations from the middle and end of Chapter One of *Moral Education:*

What can we do about it? What ought we to do? There are those who, perhaps understandably, want to reverse the trend, to drag society back to a more 'stable' era of relative peace, of generally accepted norms and mores, to a time of non-debate with the liberal use of words such as 'blasphemous', 'obscene', 'unforgivable', 'unthinkable', 'censored', 'unmentionable', and so on. Some such people believe that this can be done by identifying and preserving standards, by strengthening law and order, by prescribing, by introducing new regulations and laws, by devising new penalties, by keeping out 'alien' influences and ideas, by censoring.[52]

Perhaps in closing this chapter we may make a plea for tolerance? It is inevitable that in a belatedly and rapidly developing area of the curriculum such as 'personal education' there will be conflicting ideas about what should be done, how it should be done and what the priorities are — which is why research is so important. Let us accept that little empires will be built, some of which we may not personally like. We can at least show that we really care about children and try to put their interests first by being much more careful about the destructive attacks which we launch upon work which is not in our area and which we may therefore imperfectly understand and towards which we may not be sympathetic. In presenting our own approaches we are usually much more reliable than we are in rejecting others' work. There are no universal authorities in this field, too many factors are relevant to moral and social education. As long as we submit approaches to be used with children to discussion and trial there is little to fear if we believe that truth is self-authenticating. Teachers sensitive to the responses of their children and children's parents and their colleagues should not be fearful of trying what they judge to be potentially useful. It is easy to sit in the background criticising the efforts of others. It is more mature, courageous and helpful having identified a need to try to meet it.[53]

## Notes

1. M. Eraut *et al*, 'The Analysis of Curriculum Materials', University of Sussex Education Area Paper No. 2.

2. Aristotle, Rhetoric, II. xxi.2, cited in Dixon P., *Rhetoric,* (Methuen & Co., London, 1971), p. 14.

3. Schools Council, *Moral Education in the Secondary School,* (Longmans, London, 1972), p. 3. Henceforth referred to in the text as *Moral Education.* The book was written by P. McPhail *et al.*

4. I stress some paragraphs later that I do not intend to use any privileged knowledge of the research so these remarks are simply those of an outsider who has never seen *any* proposals in education or sociology which are anywhere near being logical entailments of data. Indeed some philosophers would hold that entailments as between facts and proposals are impossible. Certainly not many methodologists would reckon them likely. For sceptical literature see A.V. Cicourel, *Method and Measurement in Sociology,* (Free Press, New York, 1964).

5. I use this term deliberately loosely at this stage. What I count as rhetoric becomes clear by the end of the chapter. It is not a term of abuse.

6. I do have some 'inside' knowledge of one project, Schools Council Project Health Education 5-13, (Nelson, London, 1977). I do not make significant use of it.

7. Schools Council, *Moral Education*.

8. One cannot of course observe length. One sees thickness and uses a knowledge of publishing formats and of the subject to work out not only rough numbers of pages but length (perhaps) of time to read. Length, like many superficially physical measurements, turns out to have both social and metaphorical aspects.

9. The discussion of prefaces and indeed the whole of this book owes an incalculable debt to the work of the late Harvey Sacks. Education readers who are unacquainted with Sacks's work will find Coulter's appreciation useful, J. Coulter, Harvey Sacks, 'A Preliminary Appreciation', *Sociology,* Vol. 10, (1976), pp. 507-12.

10. I use the term following Tarski in A. Tarski, *Logic, Semantics and Meta-Mathematics, Papers from 1923 to 1938,* (Oxford University Press, London, 1969), p. 153.

11. A term used by Garfinkel and Sacks. H. Garfinkel and H. Sacks, 'On the Formal Structures of Practical Actions' in J.C. McKinney and E.A. Tiryakian (eds), *Theoretical Sociology: Perspectives and Development,* (Appleton-Century-Crofts, New York, 1970).

12. Of course we know things about a text that do not come out of it. Once the text has given us a few clues we can bring into play a host of understandings about books, curriculum texts etc. which are as it were activated by this text. These help us to make sense of the text.

13. In addition to 'outside' knowledge (see previous note) we can go elsewhere in the text in order to understand a piece of it. Most obviously we use early pieces to understand later ones. Less obviously we reinterpret early ones in the light of later ones.

14. These two methods of 'repairing' indexical expressions are only separated for explanation. They are really one.

15. For an exception see D.C. Anderson, 'Some Organisational Features in the Local Production of a Plausible Text', *Philosophy of the Social Sciences,* (8), pp. 113-35.

16. I do not imply that publishers hold theories of rhetoric nor that assumed theories lie 'behind' their talk about titles and such matters. It is I who capitalise on their talk.

17. Bishop Berkeley wished to get at such 'bare notions'. I.A. Richards discusses the futility of such a wish in I.A. Richards, *The Philosophy of Rhetoric,* (Oxford University Press, New York, 1965), p. 5.

18. Further discussion of this futility (see previous note) occurs throughout this book.

19. See Anderson, 'Some Organisational Features . . .', and H. Sacks, 'On the Analysability of Stories by Children', in J.J. Gumperz and D. Hymes, *Directions in Sociolinguistics: the Ethnography of Communication,* (Holt, Rinehart and Winston, 1970).

20. C. Bell, (ed.), *Inside the Whale, Ten Personal Accounts of Social Research,* (Pergamon, London, 1978).

21. D. Smith, 'K is Mentally Ill: the Anatomy of a Factual Account', *Sociology,* Vol. 12, No. 1 (1978).

22. D.C. Anderson and W.W. Sharrock, 'Irony as a Methodological Convenience', in E.L. Wright (ed.), *Irony,* (Harvester Press, London, in press, 1980).

23. D.C. Anderson and W.W. Sharrock, 'Biasing the News: Technical Issues in Media Analysis', *Sociology,* 8, (1979), pp. 376-85.

24. It is important to state that this ironic contrast is often not explicit. Sometimes it is the sheer quantity of materials and words which imply that the existing situation is inadequate. In the case of *Moral Education,* the particular paragraph cited is far from critical to the argument. But throughout the book the ideas of interpersonal relations and moral education, and of the belief that moral behaviour is rewarding, are announced as if they were *news:* as if they were not already accepted.

25. Schools Council Health Education Project, 9-13, (Nelson, London, 1977), Introduction.

26. D.C. Anderson, 'Borrowing Other People's Facts', paper given at the British Sociological Association Annual Conference, University of Warwick, (1979).

27. Schools Council/Nuffield Foundation, *The Humanities Project: an Introduction,* (Heinemann, London, 1970), p. 3.

28. Ibid., p. 9.

29. Schools Council, *Mass Media and the Secondary School* (Macmillan, London, 1973), p. 3.

30. Schools Council, *Moral Education,* p. 12, and citations, pp. 21-2.

31. Ibid., p. 18.

32. Idem.

33. Ibid., p. 5.

34. Dixon, *Rhetoric,* Chapter Three.

35. Schools Council, *Moral Education,* p. 5.

36. Ibid., p. 5.

37. Ibid., p. 5.

38. Ibid., p. 6.

39. Ibid., pp. 5-6.

40. Schools Council, *The Humanities Project,* p. 3.

41. Ibid., p. 3.

42. Their commonness is known largely through personal communication.

43. This is not strictly true. There is an option that it could be 'translated' for practitioners if a third party in-service training programme is mounted.

44. Expressed in the wish of innovators not to be thought of as writing 'tips' for teachers.

45. And possibly of the school organisation and the local 'community'.

46. H. Garfinkel, *Studies in Ethnomethodology,* (Prentice Hall, Englewood Cliffs, 1967).

47. D.C. Anderson and W.W. Sharrock, 'A Sociology of Directional Hospital Signs', *Information Design Journal,* Vol. 1, No. 2, (1979).

48. See Schools Council, *Religious Education in Primary Schools,* (Macmillan, London, 1977).

49. H. Garfinkel and H. Sacks, 'On the Formal Structures of Practical Actions' in J.C. McKinney and E.A. Tiryanian (eds), *Theoretical Sociology: Perspectives and Developments,* (Appleton-Century-Crofts, New York, 1970).

50. Garfinkel, *Studies in Ethnomethodology.*

51. Dixon, *Rhetoric,* Chapter Three.

52. Schools Council, *Moral Education,* p. 10.

53. Ibid., p. 21.

# 3 THE DEVELOPMENT OF ARGUMENT

## Introduction

This chapter considers some of the ways in which authors develop their
arguments. It uses, as an illustrative basis, the Humanities Project
Introduction.[1] As with other texts, the comments are about this one
text and do not refer to anything else the project produced.

The introduction has 59 numbered pages but 22 of these are
appendices. The body of the introduction is 36 pages. As I shall only
be able to deal with some small excerpts of these, I will first sketch out
the overall heading plan of the booklet and summarise the topical
development of the argument, adding some notes about forms.

## Heading Plan

In the following plan (a) is a heading inclusive of (b) which is inclusive
of (c) etc. (a) is in bigger type or heavier type than (b) and (b) than
(c) etc.

(a)    The Humanities Project
(b)    Introduction
(c)    1. The raising of the school leaving age
(c)    2. Humanities for the adolescent: the problem
(c)    3. The point of departure of the Humanities Project
(c)    4. Controversial issues and professional ethics
(c)    5. The outlines of an experimental teaching strategy.
(c)    6. The materials
(d)      Using the materials
(d)      The nature of evidence
(d)      Films in humanities work
(d)      Extending the collection
(c)    7. Understanding discussion in the classroom
(d)      (i) Who talks to whom?
(d)      (ii) Which people take part in the discussion?
(d)      (iii) Who leads?
(d)      (iv) Is there a concern to involve everyone?

**Topical Development**

Under the sub-heading 'Introduction' up to the first sub-sub-heading 'The raising . . .', the authors announce their introduction as an *interim* report accompanying some first materials, a report to encourage teachers to experiment using it as a platform, and a report founded on the following premises:

1. that controversial issues should be handled in the classroom with adolescents;
2. that the teacher accepts the need to submit his teaching in controversial areas to the criterion of neutrality at this stage of education, i.e. that he regards it as part of his responsibility not to promote his own view;
3. that the mode of enquiry in controversial areas should have discussion, rather than instruction, as its core;
4. that the discussion should protect divergence of view among participants, rather than attempt to achieve consensus;
5. that the teacher as chairman of the discussion should have responsibility for quality and standards in learning

After emphasising the element of discussion generally in the book and pointing out the index, the section stops. The next section then starts off immediately talking about the school-leaving age. Clearly from this

section's name, topic and heading type we can see that the previous
section has been an introduction to the whole book. The explicit argument starts in the school-leaving section. There it is argued that the
raising of the school-leaving age may increase the number of 'reluctant
students' at school or the extent of their reluctance. These problems
will sometimes be beyond the ability of the school but some of them
are within the school's potential. Obstacles to the school's more
effective handling of them include 'the entrenched attitude of some
teachers'[2] but they also include pedagogical problems. Teachers need
new knowledge and techniques and 'this is the justification for research
and development in curriculum and teaching.'[3]

'Humanities for the adolescent' defines the humanities as the arts,
religion, history and the behavioural sciences, and notes the quality
of controversy that they share, and the susceptibility of these subjects
to the problems of alienation and the reluctant student. The next
section explains the origins of the project set up to offer research
support and materials in these difficult areas. It concludes with a list of
issues selected by the project and a justification of their choice. The
next section returns to the issue of controversy and looks at ways it
might be handled, arguing for 'neutrality'[4] as the best response. This
'raises' the issue of how to actualise 'neutrality' as a teaching technique
which, in turn, leads into Section '5' on experimental teaching strategy.
The strategy outlined needs materials and further advice on chairing
and discussion techniques which take up sections '6' and '7'-'11'
respectively. The titles of Sections '12' to '14' explain their content
well enough.

Very crudely these sections can be organised as follows:

'1' describes an educational problem, the 'reluctant student'
'2' describes a humanities problem connected to 'the reluctant student'
'3' specifies the project's scope
'4' selects a particular issue of the problems described in '1' and '2' and
   selects a particular response
'5' outlines how that response can be turned into teaching strategy

Even more crudely we can divide these into three:

Definition of the problem
Definition of the solution
Elaboration of techniques and materials involved in solution.

Again, crudely, the dynamics of the argument are:

The *alienation-controversy problem* calls for a *pedagogic reaction* which should be *discussion-chairmanship* which in turn will necessitate certain *evidencing materials* and certain discussing, chairing, researching *techniques.*

The shrewd reader will also note that there are at least two arguments or levels of arguments at work here. First, there is an argument about a problem that teachers are alleged to have, and a possible solution they could try out. Then there is an argument about the activities of the research team, the authors. During these pages the authors 'justify' the relevance of their work to the problems of teachers and 'explain' why *they* are producing the materials which they are and why they are doing so now. Of course it would be possible to find that the authors had argued well but that their materials were practically useless. At the same time it should be stressed that the argument is not just an argument about abstractions but about action. It is not a purely academic argument but has a touch of the salesman. 'Look, this is your problem. The solution is this..What you will need are these so we have prepared them for you. Try some of them out.'

Another way of approaching this is to note the consequences of failure. If we do not agree about the problem then not only is the solution trite but we will not be very tempted to try out the materials or to read on. We will find that as far as we are concerned the project has been wasting its time and our money. The point to be derived from all this has to do with the structure and type of several curriculum project arguments. A lot of materials, a lot of training weekends, a lot of policy change in the school and classroom are predicated on *a* problem-solution argument. If the argument is found to fail, the cost to its producers is considerable. The overall argument connects the three components: problems, solutions and materials-techniques (implementations) such that the last of these, while often the biggest (in the simplistic sense of more paper, time, etc.), is very dependant on the acceptability of the first two. In the case of the Humanities project a lot of argumentative capital is invested in the notion of controversy-neutrality. In the *Moral Education*[5] project the notions of interactive morality and the rewards of moral actions are crucial to many of the materials. In the Health Education Project[6] introductory booklet a similar role is played by 'career' and 'self-concept' and 'decision-making' and, to a lesser extent, the Piagetian introduction to the chapter we examine in *Religious Education*[7] and the preoccupation with the working class in *Mass Media*[8] are vital to the operations they underwrite. This may or may not be of any eventual consequence but it should be of *initial* interest to the would-be critical reader. For it means that some of the pages in these books repay more careful attention than others. If authors are investing a lot of argumentative capital in a couple of summarised perspectives or one central under-writing notion or a definition of a problem, then that will repay examination. For, as we shall note many times, the curriculum innovator is pressed by diverse groups expecting him to take their interests into account. He writes and researches for many recipients and he is strongly tempted to concentrate on some activities more than others. It is the job of the critic to make sure that 'lesser' components are not used to do greater argumentative work and that those components which are crucial to an argument have themselves been decisively argued. This is particularly and obviously true in linear arguments. When then I select Sections '1' to '4', especially '4', of the Humanities Project Introduction for closer inspection, the reader will not be surprised.

One curious feature of the problem-solution argument deserves attention, however, before we proceed. In the second paragraph of the book the authors list some basic premises which are cited above. They explicitly call these 'premises'. This is curious because they then go on to argue for them rather than to argue from them. I shall assume throughout this chapter that they are using 'premise' in a fairly loose way to describe not an axiom but a basis, starting point, underlying perspective, etc. The fact that they argue their 'premises' adds some weight to my interpretation but something more interesting can be made out of the premise issue. Classically, hearer/readers should accept speaker/writers' axioms and start the criticism from that point on. Their criticism should be of the deductions from the premise not the premise itself. There are, though, three occasions which are different. First, if the author is trying to make his argument not only a practical one but one for practitioners he should be as much concerned with their premises as his. Certainly they will wish to look at his, check them against their own for relevance and discontinue reading if they do not find any. Secondly, there are conventional expectations about justifying proposals. If the authors are asking the readers to take seriously the materials and techniques then the readers will be looking for a justification *sufficient* for the effort involved in so doing. Despite the presence of the word 'premises' above the list on page one, the first few sections will get read as such a justification. Thirdly, practical readers do not act very classically about premises, particularly premises such as those in the Humanities Introduction. The very type of thing that the authors put in their premises *needs* justification. In summary, with premises as with other argumentative devices, one rarely finds them in 'pure' form in natural language. Saying that something is a premise, conclusion, example, etc. is no guarantee it will or should be read as such. The reader will and should examine the context in which it appears to find what it does and what it might be reasonably expected to do.

## The Argument

### 4. Controversial issues and professional ethics

> Our current affairs lesson was horrible. We had to sit and listen to the teacher preach about what she believed.
>
> *Half Our Future,* para. 213

The crucial problem in handling human issues is that they are controversial.

By a controversial issue we mean one which divides students, parents and teachers because it involves an element of value judgement which prevents the issue's being settled by evidence and experiment.

There may be consensus among students, parents and teachers at high levels of generality, an agreement for example, that, other things being equal, war is a bad thing. In practice, this does not help the teacher since effective discussion concentrates for much of the time on specific issues which are inevitably highly controversial: should we have dropped the bomb on Hiroshima? were the two world wars justified? should the Americans be in Vietnam?

Faced with such questions in the classroom, what strategy can the teacher adopt which can be justified to parents and students? What do professional ethics demand of him?

There appear to be three possible positions open to the teaching profession.

1. A school might attempt to lay down a line to be followed by all teachers. This does not seem practicable. It would be impossible to achieve consensus on all the issues involved, and to adopt a majority decision would be to involve those teachers in the over-ruled minority in a systematic hypocrisy. Nor is it clear how the

position of the school could be justified to parents who disagreed with the majority line.

2. Each teacher might be held free to give his own sincerely held point of view. At first, this appears a much more attractive and acceptable principle, but our own observations and other research findings suggest that the inescapable authority position of the teacher in the classroom is such that his view will be given an undue emphasis and regard which will seriously limit the readiness of the students to consider other views.* It is difficult to absolve the teacher from the charge that he is attempting to use his position of authority and privilege as a platform from which to propagate his own views.

Moreover, the profession, if this view were taken, would necessarily have to commit itself to defending any teacher who urged any view on his students so long as that view were sincerely held. For example, the teacher who advocated total sexual licence or war as a means of developing masculine qualities would have to be supported by his colleagues.

This position seems untenable in practice.

3. A teacher might aspire to neutrality in teaching controversial issues. Precisely because he is aware of the bias of his own commitment, he might attempt to adopt the convention of procedural neutrality in the classroom discussion. As students often put it, the teacher may agree not to take sides in their discussion.

Even within such a convention he can, of course, never achieve complete neutrality. The important point is that he accept neutrality as a criterion by which to criticise his performance, and explain this – and the reasons for it – to his students.

This position seemed to the Project the only tenable one, yet it is often seen to have disturbing implications. Teachers may feel that they are failing students and parents if they do not give them positive advice, even though they disagree among themselves as to what that advice should be. They may also feel that the convention of neutrality on such issues threatens to emasculate them as teachers or to rob them of the rewards they value in their work.

Even if these reservations are overcome, and the criterion of neutrality is accepted, there remains the acute technical problem of devising a teaching strategy which meets the criterion of neutrality and is also effective in the classroom.

*The authority possessed by the teacher need not be equated with authoritarianism. Indeed, it is frequently built on affection, trust and respect. Most teachers seriously underestimate the power of their authority.

In spite of these problems it was felt that the arguments for the position were sufficiently compelling to suggest that the difficulties should be squarely faced. And it was possible to outline a coherent premise from which to begin.

Clearly, the position adopted by the teacher, though he accepts the criterion of neutrality in respect of controversial moral and social issues, should not be value-free. Any educational procedure necessarily implies a value position. The aim in handling controversial issues must be to attempt to devise a teaching strategy whose values can be justified in purely educational terms. The teacher's commitment is to education, not to his own views.

Educational values are represented at three levels in the work of the Humanities Project: in the selection of content, in the formulation of aim, and in the design of a teaching strategy.

The selection of certain topics for inclusion in the curriculum involves the implicit assertion that these topics are worthy of serious consideration and study, and this is a value position.

Given these topics, it is necessary to formulate an aim expressive of the purposes of teaching. The Project adopted as an aim: to develop an understanding of social situations and human acts and of the controversial value issues which they raise. To adopt as an aim, understanding, is to take a value position.

Finally, in the teaching itself certain principles must be accepted if the strategy is to be educationally justifiable. As R.S. Peters has pointed out: "education" at least rules out some procedures of transmission, on the grounds that they lack wittingness and voluntariness. It also implies certain standards. For example, education is committed to a preference for rationality rather than irrationality, imaginativeness rather than unimaginativeness, sensitivity rather than insensitivity. It must stand for respect for persons and readiness to listen to the views of others.

## The Development of Argument

The simplest way to proceed to analyse an argument such as this is to start by asking what the authors achieve at the end of it. At the end of this section the authors are able to continue 'logically' and naturally by looking at teaching strategy, producing lots of materials and suggesting skills such as chairmanship. One aspect of this achievement is to have characterised the problem-solution in such a way that it is seen to *need* these materials and skills rather than say as a problem-solution which existing materials and skills are solving anyway. Another related achievement is to have professionalised the problem-solution and the materials. It is now a problem-solution which may be dealt with by curriculum innovation, by packages of materials rather than by commonsense. This is again related to a feeling that the problem is major not in the sense of acute, but in the sense of widespread. Insofar as the argument works we are prepared by it to accept the relevance of a *collection* of materials and techniques, which are at least initially the product of a project. Put differently, the temporal organisation is present-future. The problem is now; the solution is in a few pages, over the next five years, etc. The authors do not look to the past to see how this problem has been solved. It comes over as a *new* problem. Secondly the problem-solution is *coherent* and integral. The things to which 'controversy' refers are not odd and occasional heterogeneous problems and solutions but part of a whole. It is because it is coherent and new that one might sensibly look to a research team to offer ways of dealing with it. Lastly, it is big enough and general enough to justify the scope of those materials.

Correspondingly, the critical threats to such an argument might attempt to show that while it contained 'truth', that it was in some way inadequate to justify the materials and matters which follow it. It could be inadequate in that some might claim that the problem has been around a long time, been known to be around a long time, been to a measure solved for a long time and been solved by the techniques advocated under other names. Or again the problem could be taken to pieces and shown to be lots of different issues which the term 'controversy' unsatisfactorily glosses both by collecting discrepant situations under one word and by failing to note that their discrepancy comes from their practical contexts. Similarly, the solution could be shown to be a gloss on different problems. Lastly, the generality could be challenged by pointing out both exceptions to the problem-solution and other larger problem-solutions. The combined effect of such challenges is to turn the controversy-neutrality pair into an insight and a 'tip'. Such challenges leave the 'academic' argument largely undisturbed, but by showing disjunctures between the scale of the argument and the scale of the proposal, they weaken the proposal. If they are successful the reader grants the argument but sees it as no more than a thing teachers might think about, a 'tip' and an insight. There is no more undignified fate for a curriculum innovator than to have his argument found true but trivial; to have his materials plundered for 'useful tips', his perspectives telescoped into a one sentence maxim 'Don't be judge-mental'.

The important task for the authors is to retain their significance and to avoid trivialisation. I suggest that this is in fact rhetorically more important than bringing off an entirely logically convincing argument. If one is conducting not only an academic argument but one designed to justify goods (materials and techniques and policies) that one wishes readers to adopt, then clearly a reader judgement that the argument is sound but in someway insufficient to justify the goods or the scale of goods proposed, is most damaging. Better an argument about which the reader has reservations but about whose stature and significance he has no doubt, than being right and trite. The character of the argument turns on the identity of the arguers as members of a research project and on the identity of the purpose which is providing useful orientations and materials for teachers. The argument should be seen as an argument-for-a-proposal. Its judgement is about whether it is good enough for the proposal, not just whether it is good, and its concerns are to maintain an importance and significance which will justify the scope and type of the proposals.

Three elements that we might start examining in the maintenance of significance are novelty, integrity and size.

## (a)    *Novelty*

One does not have to be an insider to know that the constellation of topics variously known as general, liberal or social studies, as current or civic affairs, or whatever, has long been seen as problematic. The project prefers to call the constellation the 'Humanities' but a list of topics given (p. 7) is

war; education; the family; relations between the sexes; poverty; people and work; living in cities; law and order; and race relations.

These are obviously themes which can draw on a range of arts and social science disciplines and the materials which the project offer on them are new. These are not the points at issue. What is crucial is that these sorts of topics have well known problems: problems to do with lack of vocational application; with academic low status; problems of associa-tion with compensatory curricula, curricula for those who have failed to get on examination tracks; problems of low esteem among teachers

resulting in less than optimal staff and timetable allocation; problems of
trendiness and fashion; problems of relevant assessment.

The actual nature of the problems is not at issue here although we
should note that the controversy problem is but one of them. My
interest is in the fact that the problematic status of these topics is well
known and has long been known. The problems are not new ones. But
not only have these problems been known for a long time, so have the
particular problems of alienation and controversy isolated by the
project. Any teacher knows there are 'touchy' subjects. Every teacher
knows there are 'reluctant' pupils. In their daily activities teachers
attempt to solve these problems both on an *ad hoc* basis and by
meetings, course-planning modifications, etc. They have tried out
solutions to the problems. One solution they sometimes use is 'not to
preach', 'to allow proper debate', 'to present both sides', 'not to be
judgemental' and so on. This is not to say that they practise neutral
chairmanship in the way and to the extent that the authors propose. It
is simply to note that the idea that controversy is a problem and that
techniques of neutrality may be the answer on occasions is as old as sin.

Yet none of this appears in the text under examination. Instead the
problem and solution are topicalised. First the argument does not start
by setting the discussion of problems and solutions into the historical
context of past pedagogic solutions. It starts with 'the raising of the
school leaving age'. From this the authors argue that the scale of the
problem will increase and thus imply the relevance of curricular
proposals 'now'. The problem is, at least in this sense, 'new'. It is also
new in that the alienation of some adolescents is thought to increase
with age, at least by some, and in that older dissatisfied pupils may
present more acute disciplinary problems. The solution is also new in
the sense that perhaps discussion techniques are more feasible with
fifteen than with fourteen-year-olds. Thus in no way do I wish to
suggest that the problems and possibilities for solutions have not
changed and developed. I simply insist that in other ways the problems
and solutions are well known and very elderly. It is only commonsense
that policy proposals are not usually entirely new. Why should they be?
No teacher or reader would expect a curriculum proposal to be entirely
new. Indeed it is impossible to envisage anything entirely new. What
concerns the reader-consumer is that the problems and solutions be
*new enough* to justify reading on to the materials-skills section and
possibly to justify consuming these materials and skills as teachers.

The authors' argument does not help these concerns. In Section '4'
(counting the present perfect as a present tense) there is no past tense

at all (excepting 'seemed to the project'). Talk is of the current problem and of possible solutions. In the discussion of solutions to the controversy problem, the three positions are expressed as 'open to the teaching profession'. In them schools 'might' do things, consensus 'would' be impossible. The profession 'would necessarily' . . . 'if this view were taken' . . . 'Teachers who advocated . . . would have to . . .' and so on. There is nothing sinister about this. The authors are free to use tenses and moods as they wish and here they are trying to abstract three model positions to help the reader see, in an economic way, the alternatives. But, if you will, as a by-product the argument finds itself talking about conditional hypothetical and subjunctive solutions to present eternal or conditional problems. All reference to past solutions and problems is cut out. What is happening is a very familiar by-product of 'academic' argumentation. To clarify 'logical' relations, practical activities are abstracted into new, conditional relationships. The talk is about what could or might be done. It is about what is open to us. It is not about what we did yesterday and today. Moreover the discussion of the favoured option, neutrality, is continued in conditional and subjunctive moods as if no one had ever done it. Notably also the authors say:

> there remains the acute technical problem of devising a teaching strategy which meets the criterion of neutrality.

as if no one has ever done such a thing.

It is important to be clear about this. It may be that the authors are merely setting up a *logical* chain which consists *first* of identification of the problem, *next* of identification of the solution, *next* of acceptance of the solution when 'reservations are overcome' and *last* of the technical implementation of the solution. Their materials, of course, fit into that chain as a real future possibility for teacher-readers. At any event the way they organise their argument is about possibilities and the future as related to their project. They do not for instance write:

> There are three ways in which teachers have responded to the controversy issue.
> 1. Some schools in Xshire have attempted to lay down a line etc . . .

At the same time it is not that they deny the fact that some teachers already do what they are proposing. It is simply that the proposal is offered as if it were new. The form in which the arguments are presented is not such as to provide resources for the reader to assess whether the proposal is sufficiently new, nor do the arguments alert him to ask critical questions about novelty. And these are the important things to note. Neither I nor the reader is helped by the text to ask one of the crucial critical questions about it.

## (b)  *Integrity*

The authors have a concern to maintain the integrity of the two terms, controversy and neutrality. It is important that the reader should see not a plethora of divergent and minor problems with Humanities teaching but one major issue. It is important that the readers should not see a host of different unconnected particular responses to these/this issue but one general solution and several techniques. It is important that the reader should see the problems and solutions not as common-sensical problems of interactional adaptation but as needing a change of approach, a whole package of new materials, a professional curriculum innovation. Both processes, the professionalisation of the issue and the conceptualisation of the issue are processes in which instances are collected. The reader is asked to see items of teaching and learning activities as instances of a concept in controversy or neutrality and to see the cumulation of such instances as such that they imply a major professional change.

What the authors offer the teacher-reader is a way of seeing some of his problems. They are to be problems of controversy. The early lines of Section '4' help him to fit this concept onto his problems. They do not just tell him that his problems in Humanities teaching are 'controversy' problems, they help him to fit his experiences to this concept. They help him organise a search for instances of controversy. In this text they do not do this by detailed example. The section justifying controversy as a major focus is, after all, only some 13 lines. They do not complete the search for him. They merely give him some clues.

First they do away with the term Humanities and replace it with human issues. Readers are invited to see the varying incongruities of the following formulations:

1. The crucial problem in teaching the Humanities is that they are controversial.
2. The crucial problem in teaching geography is that it is controversial.
3. The crucial problem I had in the last period was that it was controversial.

4. The crucial problem with the watching of the film was that it was controversial.

Controversy is an attribute which tends to go with some things more than others. It is applied to 'discussion' rather than to watching. It is encountered as a problem during a period but is not usually said of a period of time. It goes with certain activities or topics but not with whole academic disciplines. It is certainly not the crucial problem of the humanities or of teaching the humanities. But all these are ways of conceptualising what teachers do. They teach humanities; they teach geography; they have last periods and they show films. These formulations of teacher activity may, in certain circumstances be *adequate* descriptions of a teacher's activities such that to the question 'What do you do?' a teacher can answer 'I teach humanities/human issues/films/ thirty periods a week' etc. And in *isolation* some of them may be used interchangeably, often with little impact.

The humanities teacher can recognise the first sentence of '4' as applying to him. He is a handler of human issues if that is how they want to put it, and he can see that human issues are indeed controversial, especially since he has been given a list of some various issues above including sex relations and race relations. What might just escape him is that 'human issues' is being used in two different ways. It is being used as a partial but adequate implied descriptor of the humanities teacher and as a descriptor of activities liable to be 'controversial'. 'Human issues' may be as good a term as 'humanities' to refer to a certain group of teachers but once it is coupled with an attribute 'controversy' it is doing more than being any convenient term for, as I have pointed out, certain other terms would not work here. The second paragraph offers a similar example. Controversial issues are held to involve value judgements which prevent their being settled by evidence and experiment. This is of course true just as the controversy of issues is true. But the book is about humanities for humanities teachers and is a humanities curriculum. Paragraph Four persistently characterises humanities by terms which refer to a *part* of humanities teaching without that partial status being made clear. Thus value judgements may prevent issues being settled. They do not prevent books being read, expositions being given, taxonomies being organised, maps drawn, essays written, accounts being given, arguments formulated and so on. When one comes to think of it, whoever wanted to settle issues? Yet the text does not encourage one to come to think of it. It is arranged to help the reader see humanities teaching in terms such as 'human issues' and 'settling issues' because these fit well under its 'crucial problem' of controversy. Paragraph Three continues in the same way. It offers the reader a scheme for taxonomising his lessons. Lessons are *about* discussions of questions. These questions are justificatory questions. Manifestly the term 'discussion' is sometimes used loosely as an economic replacement for 'lesson' or 'session'. Manifestly it is stylistically fair enough to categorise different lessons as seeking to answer different questions. Manifestly one can collect a lot of human-ities material under the term justifications. But just as manifestly one could use other terms and classes. Equally manifestly these are stylistic, sleeping-metaphorical titles. As titles we accept them, making little of them. They are as good as any other. But in this argument they do significant work. It is as if the metaphors awake each other when they are in close proximity. While it is argumentatively of no importance to refer to lessons as discussions it becomes of considerable importance when discussion, justification and controversy are juxtaposed. For the authors are quite right: justification, discussion, controversy, issues and settling do go together.

It is simply that these terms have entered the text as indicators of something far bigger than this small issues-discussion component of Humanities. In the paragraph preceeding Section '4' the authors write:

> The selection of content for a Humanities curriculum should be justifiable as being educationally worthwhile. With adolescents the main emphasis will naturally fall on important human issues of widespread and enduring significance. The criterion for selection is not that students are immediately interested in such issues – though they may be – but that they ought to be interested; and the school has the task of interesting them.
>
> The following issues were selected by the Project for experimental study: war; education; the family; relations between the sexes; poverty; people and work; living in cities; law and order; and race relations.

'Issues' here is being used in the sense of topics (possibly interdisci-plinary topics). Clearly the examples of issues are topics, topics calling for an array of teaching techniques. Clearly the authors are still talking about the humanities and writing for the humanities teachers. Section '4' follows immediately on this and it too may be presumed to be talk-ing about the humanities, about lessons, and about topics. It is quite reasonable then to read Paragraph Four in this way. Yet when one does so one finds the terms and examples have all been arranged to fit the concept of controversy. That is what is rhetorical about the early lines of Section '4'. It manages to take a concept which is possibly applicable to some techniques or some parts of some lessons and organise for it to be read on an integral unifying concept of the humanities.

'Controversy' is neatly organised to pair with 'neutrality'. 'Neutrality' is the topic of the remainder of Section '4'. The importance of various paired formulations is extreme in this argument. Once we see human- ities as characterised by 'controversy' we can see at least the plausibility of 'neutrality' and from that see that certain behaviour (see Position 2, p. 75) is 'propaganda' and therefore sinful ('absolve'). We can also speak relevantly of 'laying down a line' and then of 'The over-ruled minority' in a 'systematic hypocrisy'. The discussion of the positions is organised around the notion of 'controversy'. The behaviours it describes as possible positions are not simply events that could happen in schools. They are events worked up into a sort of moral grammar.

Whether 'controversy' applies to a tiny segment of humanities work or to the whole operation it is of maximal importance and precise importance to the second part of Section '4'. The whole book is only an introductory booklet, a short report, etc. We might expect then that we should not place too much stress on individual terms. I hope that the case of 'issues' has reversed such expectations. If not, the case of controversy should. We might expect of a little booklet that 'contro- versy' was one of several possible terms; that the authors were suggest- ing that there were a range of different opinions about 'issues', that people did not always agree, that people were sometimes sceptical about other peoples' ideas. We might have thought that we could replace the first sentence of Section '4' with something like:

> One problem about human issues is that our society has a diversity
> of opinions. About some issues there is remarkable agreement,
> about others there tend to be two main views involving most people
> and a few who do not agree with either. Some people are fairly
> apathetic about many things. Yet often people will have different
> views based on the same standards. What is of importance is that,
> up to a point, society does divide views into differing-but-conven-
> tional and differing-and-beyond-the-pale. All this diversity does not
> prevent both alliances and considerable amounts of concerted action
> (especially in voting), talk and understanding. All in all there is
> agreement, alliance, cooperative diversity, apathy, and conflictive
> diversity.

If it is not evident from the first part of Section '4' that this would not do for the authors it becomes so in the second part. They wish to play up the conflictive, the dialectical, the oppositional. Only with these can one start talking about laying down lines, hypocrisy and propaganda as easily as they do. If we try out my formulation about societal variation then Position 1 becomes:

> When teachers do occasionally find problems with divergent views they could well meet and while not attempting to precise one view, they might well decide a range of views which they are prepared to subscribe to, arguing that beyond that range or alliance the school could not be expected to cater. While respecting the total freedom of conscience of all teachers and pupils, they could recognise together that discussion is a practical activity in which certain things have to be ruled out for all sorts of reasons.

and we could re-write Position 2:

> many teachers are aware of the representativeness of their own views and in some circumstances and with due cautions will wish to give them. They have always done so. If they do not do so, pupils will infer them anyway. They should of course use their commonsense in such matters. Given the complex distribution of views referred to above, it is obvious that giving one's views in many circumstances does not amount to propaganda and is in no need of absolution. Because views are not simply oppositional, the profession would not have to commit itself to 'defending' such a teacher. Usually neither defence nor attack would ensue. If anything ensued it would be far more sophisticated and covert than 'defence'. In practice most teachers know what would be silly views to advocate even if curriculum innovators do not think they do.

The authors' arguments for neutrality are derived from the characteristic of controversy. They posit two reactions to controversy which are, given their meaning of controversy, untenable. This enables them to move on to a third — 'neutrality' — which they opt for. That in turn enables them to justify their materials and techniques. I have argued that their concept of controversy is not applicable to the Humanities but to a tiny part of it and that they manage not to draw attention to this by the way they arrange terms in the early stages of Section '4'. I have further argued that they make the term 'controversy' do a great

deal of work. They use it in a very precise sense so as to invalidate the
two possible reactions I have outlined and in order to derive a moral
grammar with which to abuse the two reactions. It is not that my
characterisation of the distribution of views is better than theirs. It is
that their's is both totally unjustified and unevidenced and is rhetorical,
being far more argumentatively influential than it is announced to be.
If the authors had argued for a precise and explicit state of controversy
then disagreement could have been about that. The criticism is in this
case about the significant work done by apparently casual and fairly
trivial terms such as 'controversy' and 'issues'. What is ironic is that this
work is to make appear significant what I feel is a trivial observation
about social views, and teaching in the Humanities.

Readers will also notice that by the end of Section '4' the orientation
of the authors to neutrality has become, via the discussion of other
positions, a position rather than, say, an insight.

(c)   *Size*

Our discussion is of how the authors manage to make their suggestions
about controversy-neutrality important enough to justify the proposals
about materials and techniques they wish to make. So far I have argued
that they do this by playing up the novel in their argument or rather
cutting out possible ties with the familiar and by portraying their
suggestion as one about the 'humanities' rather than about a few techniques, and as about an innovative concept rather than commonsense.
These are related to a final but wider consideration; that of size.

Size is an important but extremely elusive feature of natural
language arguments. When critics talk of 'a major contribution to
education' or when curriculum innovators abjure 'just offering tips
for teachers in favour of . . .', the issue of what I crudely refer to as
'size' is raised. Size does have a physical component. There are a number
of people in a research project, a number of pages in a project book, a
number of pupils to be affected by the curriculum proposal, a number
of evidences given and so on. There is also a sense of proportionality.
You need so much evidence for such an argument which will justify this
amount of change in schools for which that number of materials will be
needed. While it would be difficult for us to be explicit about what
constitutes acceptable proportionality, there are circumstances in which
the recipient of a proposal will find that the evidence is 'too flimsy'
for the conclusion, or that the innovator has a point 'but his suggestions
go *too far*'.

Obviously the innovator who wants lots of changes made in schools or who has lots of materials to sell will wish to show that his reasons are big enough to support these. We have already seen that one way something can be made bigger is by portraying parts as wholes or simply by not providing the resources for a reader to see the extent of the partiality of the concepts and innovation in a project. Novelty too has to do with size. If a suggestion can be shown to be 'new' then its proponents can point to its uniqueness, it is *'all* there is'. More important, it becomes problematic to compare its size with other proposals. It cannot be seen as only a small extension of some other thing. Novelty can cut out the possibility of threatening and belittling measurements. There are some other ways in which cases may be inflated.

In Section '4' the problem is identified as controversy and it is identified more precisely as a *practical* problem confronting the teacher faced with certain issues — 'should we have dropped the bomb on Hiroshima?' etc. It is worth saying that this is not a practical issue. The characteristic of practical action is that it occurs in a complex context of time, place, condition, restrictions, possibilities, etc. *Practical* problems are not problems such as how to respond to an 'issue' but how to respond to this question from that student at this time given that the last pupil has just said this and that the pupil at the back is loudly doing that. We may take the notion of practice seriously and not just as a way of introducing a problem reformulation by making *one* change in the context as do the authors. They take a problem 'war' and note that in practice it may be a particular war that is discussed. This permits them to get over the obvious fact that people often agree about things by reformulating the problem into topical instances which many people do not agree about (Hiroshima, etc.). If we do take the notion of practice seriously, it obviously undermines this sort of problem reformulation. Indeed, it threatens the authors' whole argument. First the practical problem of the teacher is not one topical issue, controversial or not and general or not, but a complex of matters. These include elegant attention to the this's and that's which make up classroom interaction. If we wish to abstract some which may be particularly prominent in this sort of lesson they may have to do with how 'I got to take this class with that boy on a Friday afternoon when . . .'. They may have to do with apathy, staff allocation, the relation to other parts of the timetable, to personalities, to choice of room, to the vocational aspirations of pupils, to what we did last week as much as to controversy. The notion of controversy as *the crucial problem* can only be maintained in the argument if the terms of the argument are kept at a level of abstraction which shades out the actual contingencies of practical classrooms. This is the level at which the authors, like so many curriculum innovators (see Chapter Six) work. The words 'in practice' should not then be taken too literally. The authors have no intention of attending to the complexities of practice at least at this stage. They only use the 'in practice' device as a way of reformulating a consideration potentially damaging to their argument into one which supports it.

After that they not only return to a high level of abstraction but they increase the level and use it to great rhetorical effect. Their teachers are not 'faced' with 'questions like these *in the classroom'*. And in response to them the teachers do not *do actions,* they *adopt positions.* The first group of teachers do not do things, instead an abstraction, the school, performs a function 'lay[ing] down a line'. The second group do not say actual things. They are 'held free to give' their own sincerely held views. This is of course legitimate abstractive writing. The reader, particularly the practical reader, fills in the practical instances of the abstractions. He completes and instances the authors' argument. If he is a teacher he can see a group of teachers meeting to work out their 'line on soft drugs' or he can see that fool Harris trying to persuade IV C to be vegans. How much more sensible, he may agree with the authors, to do what they suggest. But what do they suggest? In this context they imply that it is better *not* to work out a line or give one's views. In this context, i.e. one of contrasting three approaches, their position is *not* to do things, not to hold meetings and not to proselytise. This sensible negative suggestion is inflated into something which emerges from nowhere called the 'convention of neutrality'.

This is obviously no simple suggestion to avoid two sorts of action. This is a technique. Within half a page we find the following:

'A teacher might aspire to neutrality'
'he might attempt to adopt the convention of "procedural neutrality" '
'within such a convention'
'the important point is that he accept neutrality as a criterion'
'They may also feel that the convention of neutrality'
'and the criterion of neutrality is accepted'
'a teaching strategy which meets the criterion of neutrality'
'the criterion of neutrality in respect of controversial moral and social issues'

The argument has posed a classroom problem and suggested a solution to it. This solution is formulated and intensely repeated in such a way as to make the reader feel that there is a 'thing', a technique, an approach or a method 'the convention of procedural neutrality'. The level of abstraction in the argument has enabled the authors to conclude it, not with a tip, not with a sensible suggestion, but with an approach. This is itself generative in an inflationary way. The sensitive reader can anticipate perhaps the materials and advice to come. If the solution is 'to adopt the convention of procedural neutrality' that suggests other domains such as debates, courts and enquiries, other functions such as chairmen. It suggests that books can now be 'evidence'. Classes can be seen as 'groups' with all the potential problems of groups. Indeed all the resources of group work can now be seen to be relevant to the classroom. Nothing in the classroom will be the same again. This is a major re-orientation.

Throughout the 1960s teachers were invited to see their work from a bewildering number of metaphorical 'perspectives'. Why not consider the teacher's role as one of social control? Conceive of the lesson as consisting in aims, objectives and strategies! The classroom is a market place in which teachers and pupils negotiate. Learning is taking a series of decisions. The classroom is a microcosm of the social world. These are metaphors and those which are good metaphors help the teacher see the classroom in new ways. They are not models. They abstract certain features from teaching, clean them of their practical context, shade and intensify them for impact then offer them to teachers. Seen as metaphors they are essentially inventive but brief. They are invitations to see familiar ground in a new way. One can get the hang of them quickly and build oneself on them. Their crucial features are inventiveness, brevity, and optionality. Their producers are to be congratulated on being the first to see things the way they did or on being able to express them cogently and enticingly. But the producers need not be tarried with. Once the practitioner has grasped the metaphor he can build and develop it himself. Moreover he will know that the practical working situation is not an instance of the metaphor, that the metaphor is only one of a large number of ways of looking at the classroom or whatever and that 'looking at it' and running it are distantly related matters.

The Humanities Project authors do not present their work like this. No more indeed do the Marxists, interactionalists and decision-makers listed above. They want more than to be the makers of inventive metaphors. Some dream of systems, others of major change. They inflate their arguments by a number of devices and use them, once inflated, to call for shifts in whole areas of the curriculum, or to justify lots of 'new' materials, or to redirect teacher education. In the case of the Humanities Project Introduction book this inflation is achieved by a sustained formulation of 'problems', 'solutions' and proposals which presents these in a proportionally acceptable way. This involves the formulation of the argument as new, or at least not familiar, the problem and solution as whole fields of activities and the solution as a method rather than a metaphor.

## Notes

1. Schools Council/Nuffield Humanities Project, *The Humanities Project: an Introduction,* (Heinemann, London, 1970)
2. Ibid., p. 4.
3. Idem.
4. Ibid., pp. 7-8.
5. Schools Council Project, *Moral Education in the Secondary School* (Longmans, London, 1972).
6. Schools Council Health Education Project, 5-13, (Introductory booklet). (Nelson, London, 1977).
7. Schools Council Project, *Religious Education in Primary Schools: Discovering an Approach,* (Macmillan, London, 1977), pp. 13-25.
8. Schools Council Research Study, *Mass Media and the Secondary School.* (Macmillan, London, 1973).

The extract on pp. 74-6 is reproduced by permission of the Schools Council from *The Humanities Project - an Introduction.* The Schools Council/Nuffield Humanities Project available from CARE, University of East Anglia, Norwich NR4 7TJ

# 4 PRESENTING RESEARCH

## Introduction

Consider research provisionally as a collection of cognitive activities.[1]
Consider it as analyses, taxonomies and theories. It is in the nature of
such cognitive activities that they are secret — known only to their
owner. These ideas, theories, analyses, etc. can persuade no one until
they are spoken or written, that is no one apart from their owner. But
when they are spoken or written they are presented both in a literary
context, i.e. on a page, in a book, in a discussion, in a monologue and
in a social context for this audience, as a seminar, to help with curriculum change, etc. If such presented research persuades, it is always an
issue whether the persuasion be achieved by the research itself,[2] by the
management of the literary or social context or by an alleged relationship between the two. If research is ideas then, as I.A. Richards pointed
out, it is as slippery as an oiled Indian thief.[3]

Some curricular comments and proposals announce themselves as
'research' in their titles. On the inside of *Mass Media in the Secondary
School*[4] (the text considered in this chapter and henceforth referred to
as *Mass Media*) we find that it is one of the series 'Schools Council
Research Studies'. Other curriculum texts announce their research
identity in the text:

> This general introduction to the Humanities Project is an interim
> report on a programme of continuing research and development.[5]

Others may not use the word 'research' but point to a prolonged
series of activities which are used to underwrite the book, activities
connected with institutions which do do research:

> This book is the result of a project on religious education in primary
> schools sponsored by the Schools Council and based at the University
> of Lancaster.[6]

Yet others point out their 'research' activities and list them along with
other evidences:

91

The units represent areas of health concern which the project team through its researches and work with teachers has come to recognise as basic to a school health education programme.[7]

Apart from these concise announcements, the nature of the comments and suggestions which various curriculum project authors make, the frequent textual references to their experiences prior to the writing of the book, the mention of a large number of articles and persons understood by the simplest reader to be connected with research, and in some cases the presented identity of the authors themselves combine to produce a general claim, and a sustained and important claim that the book is connected with research. Some of the components of that claim are:

1. The authors have done *work* prior to and *distinct from* the writing of the book.
2. That work was of a potentially high quality. In its academic depth or in its more than local scope, in its sponsorship (Schools Council) and financing and its presentational form (a published book), it far exceeds what the individual reader-teacher can do.
3. This work was not isolated. It was part of a 'programme' or 'project'.
4. It was not individual or idiosyncratic but undertaken by a group, a 'team', 'we', 'The members . . .' etc.
5. The book is the 'result of' or is based on the research.
6. This basis is not trivial but central.

Apart from generally enhancing the author's authority by collecting him in good company, showing sustained work, distancing the reader from the topic and all the other things noted in Chapter Two, this composite claim sets the rhetorically alert reader a general puzzle and some particular puzzles.


## Puzzles

If seminars, lectures, articles, and books, etc. are not research 'itself' but versions of research, presentations of research, accounts of research, where is the real thing 'research' to be found? More precisely, is the research of curriculum projects available in any form, that is, any public form, which does not affect 'the research'? Is the model suggested by the curriculum projects and provisionally considered at the start of this chapter, a model which suggests there are two things 'research' and 'the book based on research' (or the seminar, lecture, report, etc. based on research), a reasonable one? A moment's thought will reveal that, while we might wish to say that research is a cognitive activity, there is no-where anything which can be identified as 'this' research in 'this' instance. Quite simply, in the case of a research team who do not have access to the contents of each other's heads independently of each other's presentations of that content, and probably in the case of individual research, to speak of public versions based on research is at best to speak metaphorically, at worst sloppily. There is no such thing as research, at least no such thing available to self and other later. There are only accounts of research, rememberings of research, tales of research, tabulations of research, all of which have forms. These forms are designed to do practical jobs for certain reader/hearers. They are practical, thus my rememberings are for my purposes in writing this report, in explaining to this funder or that practitioner that proposal where their status as a practical this and practical that affects the research reports. None of this is to suggest that at any time there is only the research as it is presented at that time. There are of course tables, records, logs, diaries and past tales and reports. What there is not is research-free-of-practicality. What there is not is one sure and boundaried 'it' – the real thing. So what?

The most important implication of this is that the research/report dichotomy, while not logically sustainable, is of tremendous rhetorical use. It gives the author a sure 'it' which *he* knows, indeed which he produced, but to which the reader cannot have access. The 'actual research' would be too long, too complicated too irrelevant so the reader is presented with a special version which is more suitable. Of course this version is 'only' a version. And the reader should not judge it as the 'real thing' but treat it as an icon standing for the real thing. Since the reader is assured that there is a 'real thing' there is no sense in the author duplicating it in the book. The author has extreme licence to 'select' the most important 'findings' of the real thing and give the reader an *account* of how the research got done. In a very important rhetorical sense, the constitution of and the plausibility of the research are products of the book not vice versa.

Reading a curriculum project book and trying to analyse it, aware of this general puzzle, is like fighting an image in a hall of mirrors. Standard methodology just has not addressed the issue of how to analyse the research worth of a document which

(a)    claims not to be research but 'based' on it
(b)    in keeping with that claim is constructed in its own right as a book, manual, etc.
(c)    claims for its authors privileged access to 'real research'
(d)    thus meaning that only the authors can know if the relationship between the 'real research' and the document is satisfactory.

Readers faced with this hall of mirrors can adopt one of two responses. Either they can do the methodological equivalent of smashing one of the reflecting mirrors. They can wait for the rare moment when they do have a piece of sustained data and argument, smash into it and judge the whole book on the basis of it. Or they can trust the author provided he shows an awareness of research 'front' and parades out his response levels, his sample sizes and his methodological models. Both strategies can be observed in book reviews.

But the rhetorical use of the 'real research/version' dichotomy and the author's unique access to both and the relationship between the two, is not only of general use. Once the reader accepts that the book is to be judged as a version of something he cannot see, then he may well accept the strategic introduction of bits of the 'real research he cannot see'. These arrive in tables 'drawn from the research', in graphs, etc. As well as accepting these interpolations the reader may happily read several pages telling him the story of the research he cannot see. He will certainly welcome helpful diagrams clarifying matters he cannot read about at length.

The remainder of this chapter considers four areas of this relationship between presented research and 'research'; the interpolation of tables, graphs and other non-prose forms allegedly drawn from 'research' and in a conventional scientific format; the interruption of prose to insert an arbitrary illustrative figure; the 'explanation' of these which usually precedes or follows their interpolation or insertion; and the sections in which authors explicitly set out to give an account of their research. The examples are taken from *Mass Media in the Secondary School* not a curriculum project itself but a 'Research Study' albeit with implications for policy and for the curriculum.[8] *Mass Media* is full of all four of the types of phenomena to be considered. It has 44 listed tables drawn mostly from the authors' own researches. It has 10 figures or diagrams. Nearly all of these 54 interpolations[9] are accompanied by prose explanations. And in the appendices there are some 42 pages[10] which give an explicit account of how the research was done. Let us refer to these phenomena as *tables,*[11] *diagrams, explanations* and *accounts.*

As with other chapters I shall use one or two examples of these phenomena drawn from the text to raise some more general issues about them. In so doing, I am using the text casually, illustratively and, in one sense, unscrupulously. I do not have the space either to undertake a detailed analysis of any one table, diagram, account or explanation, or to discuss the differences between the tables, diagrams, etc. within or outside this book. The reader is reminded that the object of this exercise is not a comprehensive treatment of the rhetorical features of curriculum texts but simply the production of some initial possible tools and orientations for extending curriculum analysis into curriculum text analysis. This is important to note especially in the case of tables and diagrams. It would be a fool who would imagine that the graphical, literary, rhetorical and other features of the immense variety of tables, graphs, figures and diagrams available to the research presenter are capable of nice summary. Certainly in *Mass Media* we find, at the simplest level, differences in size. There are small tables:

**Table 2** Percentage of teachers and pupils having a TV set at home

| Teachers | Pupils |
|----------|--------|
| 83%      | 98%    |
| n 1310   | 1071   |

There are medium tables:

**Table 4** Percentages of teachers in various age groups claiming to listen to pop music 'very often' or 'fairly often'

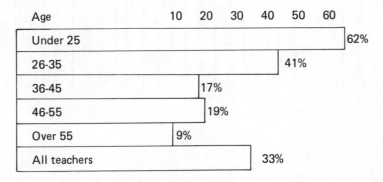

| Age | 10 20 30 40 50 60 |
|-----|-------------------|
| Under 25 | 62% |
| 26-35 | 41% |
| 36-45 | 17% |
| 46-55 | 19% |
| Over 55 | 9% |
| All teachers | 33% |

and there are tables which take up a whole page:

**Table 5** Teachers' rankings of six aspects of their job

| Job Aspect | Rankings | | | | | |
| --- | --- | --- | --- | --- | --- | --- |
| | | By type of school | | | By subject taught | |
| | All Teachers | Grammar | Comprehensive | Modern | English | Science* |
| Subject instruction | 1 | 1 | 1 | 2 | 1 | 1 |
| Moral education | 2 | 2 | 2 | 1 | 2 | 2 |
| Education in human relationships | 3 | 3 | 4 | 3 | 3 | 5 |
| Social education | 4 | 5 | 3 | 4 | 4 | 4 |
| Education for citizenship | 5 | 4 | 5 | 5 | 5 | 3 |
| Education for leisure | 6 | 6 | 6 | 6 | 6 | 6 |
| Numbers replying | 1310 | 529 | 370 | 411 | 321 | 305 |

* 'Science' is defined here as biology, chemistry, physics or general science.

There are questions which we might wish to ask of the smallest tables such as 'Why is a table being used at all?' which we might not so obviously wish to ask of larger tables. There are also obvious possibilities that whole-page and part-page tables may get read differently and related in different ways to the text. Without any more consideration than that of size, it is clear that it is *not* safe to generalise about all tables let alone all interpolations. However, there are some *common* questions that one can ask about different tables and diagrams and it is to illustrate these common questions — questions which relate to the formal[12] features of interpolations — questions about how tables are titled, where they appear in the prose text, how their items are categorised and arranged — that the examination of items from the *Mass Media* text is made. The object is then not to generate findings but some questions which it may be worth asking. For the critic of a curriculum proposal is not interested in findings but in questions, particularly awkward questions, questions whose pursuit may reduce the credibility of the text.

In turning attention towards some particular features of the *Mass Media* text, I wish to avoid two possible orientations. I do not wish, first, to criticise the research methods on which tables are 'based' and which are recounted in the 'accounts'. Secondly, I do not wish to add to the existing studies of how statistics may 'lie'.[13] I am not particularly interested in how graphs may be changed in their implications by cutting off axes at 'convenient' points; in how shading and inclination may be used rhetorically; in how argumentative capital may be made of the layers of metaphor (temporal, spatial and logical) inherent in diagrams. To discuss these tends to involve the lie detector in showing that the graph or figure *misrepresents* the research. And it consequently involves him in an interest in the research itself and an interest in what the graph or figure is *not*, i.e. the graph or figure is *not* a true representation of the data. My interest is in what the graph or figure *is*. Although overlapping, it is important to distinguish these different interests, the one in showing that certain representations are not scientific, the other in showing how they are rhetorically organised.

There is, however, one exception to my lack of interest in the data and the 'research itself'. Without any access to the actual data *re*presented in the tables of *Mass Media*; without any privileged knowledge of the actual research done behind the scenes by Murdock and Phelps; I *do* know that social science generally has methodological problems. I *do* know that there is more dispute over sociological than over chemical method. The very methods that Murdock and Phelps employ would not command the assent of some sociologists. There is open controversy about these methods.[14] There is further minimal agreement on the small body of findings which sociology may be thought to have produced. Scepticism about such matters is not confined to sociologists themselves. The 'findings' of both sociologists and educationalists on comprehensive schooling, streaming, assessment, school organisation and reading are in constant change and reversal, the source of controversy rather than the establishment of consensus. Arguments among academics, practitioners and parents rage on, this way and that. The figures which one 'side' gives to support this solution are just as easily re-interpreted to support a totally different solution by the other 'side'. One does not have to be a paid-up methodologist to see the unsatisfactory state of social science. It suffices to watch TV documentaries.

While I am not interested in the 'actual' research 'behind' *Mass Media*, I have no reason to grant it special exemption from the general state of social science, in particular sociological knowledge. I note *with* interest then that Murdock and Phelps take no notice of the widespread belief that statistics do lie, of the widespread mistrust of social science, etc. They act as if their research was the most normal, proper, agreed thing in the world. And although in their own appendix[15] they draw attention to the controversial state of method, in the body of their text they use presentational interpolations which, derived from more mature and less chaotic sciences, create an impression of solidity and consensus. I am arguing that the style of presented interpolations conflicts with the state of research, that both the recognition of, e.g. a table as a vehicle for presenting scientific findings and the propensity of a table to exclude the sentential modifiers of caution, hesitancy etc., make it a useful device for making findings more sure than they are; that the use of very conventional presentational forms fits ill in the lack of consensus about the methods which produced the contents.

## Tables

Consider again the small table mentioned above:

**Table 2** Percentage of teachers and pupils having a TV set at home

| Teachers | Pupils |
|----------|--------|
| 83% | 98% |
| n 1310 | 1071 |

Table 2 shows that, whereas 98% of the pupils we studied had a television set in their homes, only 83% of teachers did.

Small tables such as this one may be up to 600 per cent more expensive on space and paper than the same words in prose. Why are they used at all? For in this particular case not only is the message capable of being expressed in prose but it actually is expressed in prose immediately after the table! Indeed this turns out to be a common feature of small tables, that their contents are repeated in prose after them or announced in prose before them. After Table 2 we find: 'Table 2 shows that whereas 98% of the pupils we studied had a television set in their homes, only 83% of teachers did'. However, a second look shows us that the sentence is only the same as the table in the literal sense that it contains the common substantives 'Teachers', '83%', 'Pupils', '98%' etc. and that the sentence can be read as suggesting similar relationships of *pairing* and *contrast* between these substantives in the table and its title. Apart from there being components in the table that are not in the sentence, such as '*n* 1310, 1071', the distinguishing characteristics of the sentence are that it *follows* the table and that it is part of the prose text, whereas the table is interpolated from 'the research'. It can be seen to be a table drawn from 'research' and is thus to be considered 'data' 'facts' or 'results' as opposed to the prose which is an account of, explanation of and argument based on the research. The reader's *conventional* job is to react differently to the two even if they have similar components. He is more or less to accept the table, to scrutinise the prose and to examine the relation between the two. One might helpfully see table and prose as two boxes into which the author can choose to put the same same statement depending on what reaction he wants to it.

This is then a device, like many others we consider such as titles and chapter allocation, for controlling controversy, for suggesting what the issue is to be, for demarcation of criticism. While borrowing devices can do the same work of putting a point 'out of argumentative play', the cumulative effect of *lots* of tables — things which are not part of the text but grossly, obviously inserts and *all inserts from the same source*, is to remind the reader of that source and its extent. Moreover, taken with the other tables from the same source and which can be seen to deal with related categories (e.g. school, teachers, television, pop, etc.) the table can now be seen as an excerpt. The table is not just *from somewhere* else but is *part of something* else. This little table is a glimpse of the vast enterprise of research 'behind' the book. The table then is a device which may help the author successfully bring off the 'there is research and there are presentations of research' split. His book can take on an exegetical style in which the prose part explains the interpolations. These interpolations casually but cumulatively generate an awareness of the thing 'research-behind-the-book'. And this division is of enormous rhetorical benefit to the author. It allows him to make prose appear to be a *natural* sequential development from the table where in fact the interpolated table is *chosen* by the author himself. Let us call these effects the *critical* effect and the *structural* effect. By the critical effect the reader has his critical scope organised for him by the author. By the structural effect the author uses interpolations to give his book an exegetical and sequential form to his own argumentative advantage.

For the crucial point never to lose sight of is that the book is *all* the author's construction. Of course the table may be linked to other tables and activities outside the text, to a research report, a computer print out or whatever. It is in that sense not of the text but of research. But so may bits of the prose explanation. What is crucial is that *this* table, in *this* form, of *this* size, on *this* page, juxtaposed with *this* explanation, cumulated with *these* other tables, categorically, spatially and graphically organised to resemble them, to resemble natural science conventional tables, to contrast with the prose — that the management of all *this* is an author's affair and his responsibility. The conventional reader reaction to interpolation given above lets the author get away with substantial amounts of this rhetorical 'management' work unchecked and uncriticised. Expressed concisely, we must be critical about arguments *and* tabular interpolations *and* the arrangement of a text into the two.

Above, I suggested that the sentence and the inserted table have some common components and embody some similar relationships of identity and contrast, precisely the contrast between teachers' and pupils' 'having' a television set in the home. If we look at the components of the table we can see substantives later found in the sentence. We can see that the verbs of the table are, as it were, the spatial and linear arrangement. The table has explicit possessing nouns

and explicit possessed attributes. The relationships between them are
implied by lines and juxtaposition and separation. Totally missing
are any modifying adjectives or adverbs or indeed precising subordinate
clauses. In Chapter Two we noted that academic prose style is marked
by extensive use of such modifying and precising figures. It is cautious
and equivocal. Clearly small tables such as Table 2 are not cautious or
equivocal, at least not in the same way as prose. Clearly they contain
the minimum of details, exclusions, modifications, specifications, etc.
Simple tables show relationships simply, even starkly. That is one of
their 'educational' advantages. But in highlighting these relationships
they obscure others. Table 2, removed from its research home and set
in its new context, a chapter on the experiential gap between teachers
and pupils, invites the reader to see a contrast by its spatial/linear
organisation and its positioning after a preface about the experiential
gap between pupils and teachers.

> It is now generally recognised that there is a sizeable gap between
> the life experiences of many teachers and the everyday lives of
> many pupils.

(The first words of the chapter containing Table 2).
A neglected issue about arguments asserting a contrast is their
*maintenance of focus*, the techniques whereby they keep attention on
that contrast. It is important, especially in the 'social' field where it is
well known that different aspects interrelate, that we live in a pluralist
society and that there are gaps in the life experiences of different
genders, different ethnic groups, different religious groups, first and
second generation 'immigrants', different social classes, town and
country — it is most important for arguments about one or two of these
'aspects' not to allow *distraction*. The arguer's job is not only, or even
mostly, to establish that his contrast holds but that it is *the* contrast.

In this task he will find experimental and hypothetico-deductive
methods some help since they, like he, wish to restrict the number of
variables to be considered, but these methods will not be adequate both
because very restricted hypotheses are seen to be laughably crude and
because even fairly restricted ones suggest several contrasts and other
relationships. The simple table solves all this. It is well known that it
is used to help the reader. It is a stylistic device which depends on
simplicity, and simplicity is just what the arguer wants. The simple
table can be used to obscure the difference between what respondents
do or have and what they say they do or have. It obscures the

difference between events and states[16] in their lives. It cuts out the context in which the questions were asked that produced the tabulated answers. It eschews subtleties and amendments. It *fixes* firm categories in volatile social worlds. And its overall function is to help reader see only the relationship which the author wishes him to see and to see that relationship strongly, its strength deriving from its stark graphical presentation and its allusion to the firm basis or 'actual research' from which it is 'excerpted'.

Once again and to the point of nausea, none of this implies any naughtiness on the part of the author. It does not mean that the table misrepresents the survey/questionnaire. What it means is that the conventional forms of data presentation, especially interpolation and the conventional myth of research separate from and behind presented research, have rhetorical side effects. They have critical effects, structural effects and focusing effects. As with citations, 'scientific' tables just cannot be easily held down to doing *only* 'scientific' work. Tables are read just like prose *reflexively* and *generatively*. We read more than is there.

For example, Table 2 is about having television sets. Televisions are fairly lumpy, contingent sorts of things not to be wished away by Oxford philosophy. Table 2 looks fairly factual. But consider two ways of reading it. First we might read it as literally as possible: 'Percentage of teachers and pupils having a TV set at home'. But then we must read it differently. To make any sense at all of it we have to look for the point of it. Is it about any teachers? No, it is about the teachers in this study. Well, we know what the study is about, experiential gaps, so we can see that this table may be concerned with those. Is the table about teachers *and* pupils? Are they different groups on a continuum? No, the business of the day is *contrast*. Is the point of contrast the geographical location of the television sets? Is it about whether the teachers and pupils had their sets at home or watched a school set? No, it is not about 'having' sets either in the geographical sense or the proprietal sense, but about having *access* to sets. We look for it to be about *access*, about contrasting levels of access because that would plausibly relate to what was *seen* on television which in turn relates to 'life experiences'. Are we to examine the possible contrast between the relationship of adult teachers to 'home' (i.e. their home) and teenage pupils' relationship to 'home' (i.e. their parents' home) with its consequent possible contrast between the legitimate derivation of viewing from 'having' in the two cases? Certainly not. The contrast at hand; the contrast prepared for by the preceding prose and title chapter; the contrast organised by the title and maintained by the spatial and linear work of the table is the contrast between exposure or viewing rates implied by access to television.

Does this matter? That we cannot tell for we have, as readers, *no* access to the circumstances and issues cut out by the tabular representation. I cannot know whether the access-exposure implication is legitimate. I cannot know whether in the authors' own words, pupils '*do*'[17] different things with their parents' televisions to what teachers do with theirs. I cannot know about the circumstances of questioning. I cannot know the multitude of possible connections and implications the table cuts out. I can see that it is an excerpted table, but not how it is excerpted. As a reader I can read the title and table in two ways. I can read it literally as simply giving me information on percentages of teachers and pupils 'having' (whatever that means) a television in the 'home' (whatever that means) and make nothing of it all. Or I can read it generatively for implications. If I do the latter I am likely to read it for the authors' implications as substantiating, or at least attempting to substantiate, their concerns. The table is not misleading. It does not misinform. It *leads*. It informs in a single argumentative direction — the authors'. It should not then be regarded as 'data' but as a rhetorical construction; as an author's device. True, it *helps* the reader, but it helps him follow the authors' argument, not criticise it. It helps him see the authors' implications and cuts out any others he might see. The interpolated table then is not interpolated at all. It is part and parcel of the book, an argumentative, not a neutral device, a tool for *educating* the reader in the original sense of *leading him out*.

If the table looks like an interpolation, but is not that; if it looks like a factual table, but is not only that; if it looks like a part of research behind the book, but is not simply that; if it is to be seen as a rhetorical device, an author's construction; this does not mean that it is inevitably persuasive. There is a danger throughout this book that, in pointing out persuasive devices, I may be thought to be seeing them as actually persuading people. Obviously devices can fail but still be persuasive devices. Even when they fail, that failure is often both partial and repairable. For example, in this case I do not find the contrast very convincing. A contrast between 83 and 98 per cent is not that strong. But note that, whether or not, it persuades me to accept that the contrast is the matter at hand, whether or not I accept this excerpt of research, the table shows me that research has been done behind and before the book. Whether or not I believe it, I read what comes after it as a natural development of it. It is a table and I am neither surprised nor critical when I find it followed by an explanation. Whether or not I agree with it, as I read on I see it as only *a* point. Its ambivalent position in the book and its status as only an excerpt and only one of many tables, restrict the extent to which disbelief of the table extends to the book. In Chapter Two it was suggested that authors use rhetorical devices extravagantly. If the reader is not convinced by one, there are always others. Table 2 is not then a crucial hinge of the *Mass Media* argument. Its partial failure is of no great consequence, and it is a partial failure. It still has structural and critical effect.

One possible response to these suggestions is to argue that although one table may have rhetorical effect, most research presentations use many. Certainly Mass Media does and certainly we find teacher/pupil viewing hours in Table 3, and lots more evidence later on. Certainly Murdock and Phelps have worked hard. They have asked lots of questions, visited lots of schools and used surveys and interviews and graphs and fairly sophisticated analysis. But, crudely, lots of tables provide lots of opportunities for rhetorical side effects. I see no evidence that lots of tables *iron out* the effects we have noted of one table in the same way that sampling procedures iron out idiosyncrasy in survey response. Indeed, the comparison with sampling suggests the reverse. Sampling restricts methodically the choice of respondents. Whereas the author can interpolate as he wills. On each and every occasion that he inserts a table he has *licence* to decide its title, its sequential location, the number of items it will contain, how they will be formulated,[18] and so on. The presence of lots of tables will not only provide lots of rhetorical opportunities, but may alert the author to the possibility of using them serially or cumulatively, and here too he will be able to serialise or cumulate them to rhetorical advantage. Seriality can be related strongly to the structure of the book's argument. Thus, for example, when the reader readers several tables as evidencing the 'same' point, that homogeneity may well be an author's construct deriving from his titular, categorical, and chapter organisation. Further, one area in which methodology provides little guidance is how to criticise a series of interpolations. It tells us how to judge each one, but not the series.

**Explanations**

A tabular interpolation does not just occur in a block of prose splitting that block into two parts. Rather, either the preceding prose, or the following prose is read as preceding and following not only in a spatial, but an argumentative sense. Leaving aside whole-page tables and tables which are appended or which act like picture illustrations and come at any point convenient for the publisher, we find some predominant patterns in placement. Here are three from *Mass Media*:

1. ............................................. end of paragraph
   **Table title**

---
T   A   B   L   E
---

a) 'As table X shows . . .'
b) 'The most immediately striking thing about table X is . . .'
c) 'Table X illustrates the extent to which . . .'
d) 'Table X shows that . . .'
e) 'Taken overall the results shown in table X . . .'
f) 'It is obvious from these figures . . .'
g) 'The figures in table X suggest that . . .'

2. ........................................ end of paragraph
   a) 'It is evident from table X . . .'
   b) 'Table X presents the relevant findings . . .'

---
T   A   B   L   E
---

3. Start of paragraph. 'Table X shows that more teachers in grammar

---
(NEW PAGE)
T   A   B   L   E
---

schools are likely'.

Whichever format is used, overwhelmingly the authors of *Mass Media* have 'explanatory' sections in the pre or succeeding prose. By 'explanatory' I mean sections which at first sight appear to be explaining the table's significance. In fact the table and prose work are reflexively 'explaining' each other, and just as the table is not only a table, so the 'explanation' does much more than explain. During these 'explanations', the reader is told what the table shows, suggests, illustrates or evidences. The 'explanation' instructs the reader on how to read the table. This is done by repeating some of the table's components but surrounding them with a new argumentative context in which their implications for the overall argument are spelt out. A way of reading the table so as to follow and believe the argument is revealed to the reader. Tables are rarely allowed to speak for themselves. Those which occur surrounded by prose share all the characteristics of the prose. They too come in chapters, under chapter and paragraph headings, within a sustained argument, etc. and if these features do not explain the table for us sufficiently an explicit explanation is placed next to the table.

Before looking at one explanation, we might note some now familiar points. The early sections are invitations to read the table in a particular way and the expressions, 'Table X shows', 'illustrates', etc. recall the assertion discussed in Chapter Two that a book is 'the result of' research. In Chapter Five we find quotations used in such a way as to suggest they are part evidence, part illustration. Throughout all the curricular texts this book considers, this uncertainty is systematic. The books are 'based on' evidence but they are books for certain purposes and people — people who will appreciate example and illustration. The examples and illustrations are often taken from the same place, i.e. the activities of the research project and, while in the case of some anecdotes, for instance, it is clear that these are illustration and in the case of some figures that they are data, more often than not it is uncertain whether interpolations and quotes are mostly one or the other. It is not that there are two distinct things called illustrations and data. Rather, interpolations such as Table 2 have both functions. Indeed I have argued that one of their functions is to be illustrative or demonstrative *of* further unseen data. As a research author my sympathies go out to the authors of *Mass Media*. They have to write their book to satisfy fellow academics and people with policy interests in schools. Their book has to be reliable and readable. These concerns for reliability and readability affect each other particularly (but not only) in books where evidence is given *during* explanations and arguments, and given in a highly excerpted way. And if the stylistic combination of readability and reliability pose writing problems for the poor authors, they also pose criticism problems for poor readers. A felicitous combination of the two qualities makes a book pleasurable and persuasive. It makes it readable. But it makes it very difficult to criticise. Literary, argumentative and evidential activities are so enmeshed that the reader who would be critical is hobbled in several ways. He can criticise the book as if it were a scientific tract and appear unreasonable, even churlish. Does he not understand that the authors were writing a book not a research report? Or he can obscure his argument by extensive conditional prefacing 'If the authors are putting table X forward as evidence then . . .' and open himself to the charge of misreading. A traditional form of this latter tactic used in book reviews is for the reviewer to rewrite the book's argument prior to criticising it. And this is particularly open to the charge of misrepresentation. The critic is faced with the question 'What is a reasonable standard for reviewing a book which is a complex combination of evidence, example, excerpt, data, argument and suggestion?'. Some of the contortions which reviewers in education and social science journals go through are a witness to the extent of this problem. As I have repeatedly said, it is a problem with which standard methodology is minimally concerned.

Book reviewing is one of the real-life activities which might be thought to instance academic methodological scrutiny. But as a real-life activity it is not only practical but is expected to be practical and reasonable. Reviewers should bear in mind the difficulties under which researcher-authors worked, the readership for whom the book is intended, the length of the book and so on. They must review it bearing in mind that it is a book and a book produced in the imperfect social world. If they do this they may produce a *reasonable* review. Unfortunately, social scientific method seems uninterested in the practical problems of reviewers, preferring to exude methods and standards for the assessment of arguments produced in no presentational form by spectres in no world at all. The writer who wishes to make a reliable-argument-in-a-book and the reader who wishes to criticise an argument-in-a-book are engaged in very different exercises from those suggested by standard methodology and engaged in them with very little guidance.

Not only does this mean that producing academic books is a rhetorical as well as a scientific exercise; not only does it mean that individual aspects of books such as tables and quotations will contain both scientific and rhetorical features in ambivalent and volatile combinations; not only do these combinations disconcert the would-be critic, making him conditional and tentative; but they suggest that the critics who *do* make telling criticisms do so as much by the construction of their own rhetoric as by the demolition of the books they criticise. Certainly not many impressive critiques in education work by the detailed re-analysis of the data given in the books they criticise.

Let us return to the 'explanation' of 'Table 2':

**Table 2** Percentage of teachers and pupils having a TV set at home

| Teachers | Pupils |
|----------|--------|
| 83% | 98% |
| n 1310 | 1071 |

Table 2 shows that, whereas 98% of the pupils we studied had a television set in their homes, only 83% of teachers did. This figure of 83% does, of course, conceal the differences between teachers at different types of school and at various ages. Marginally fewer grammar school teachers (81%) have a television set than teachers at either comprehensives (85%) or secondary moderns (86%), but, generally, age is the more important factor. Thus, only 69% of teachers under 25 had a TV compared with 81% of those aged 26 to 35, and 91-92% of those older than 35. These differences are obviously related to the material circumstances of young teachers. For a newly qualified teacher in a bedsitter or flat, or for a young teacher starting a family, purchasing or renting a television is a luxury. However, the fact that almost a third of the teachers under 25 had little or no contact with this part of their pupils' media experience is significant, for in other respects it is the younger teachers who might have the best chance of bridging the experiential gap between themselves and their pupils. Their relative unfamiliarity with television, however, makes the establishment of common ground that much more difficult.

**Table 3** Teachers' and pupils' television viewing: mean hours per week

| | All teachers | Teachers under 25 | Pupils |
|---|---|---|---|
| Mean TV viewing hours per week | 10.0 | 8.6 | 13-20+ |

Table 3 shows that most teachers watch television far less than many of . . .

One general effect of the explanation is, in Sacks's words, to turn the table into 'something for us'. It takes the table and transforms it into a part of what we are doing here. It ties it into the argument. This is done by surrounding various of the table's components with a new context. This new context can be seen in two ways. First there are new words, not just more of the same sort, but different types of words, e.g. words modifying the terms of the table, 'only'; words contrasting the terms of the table, 'whereas'; words commenting on what is not shown in the table, 'This figure of 83% does not . . .'; words qualifying the terms of the table, 'of the pupils we studied'. The new context is also a new argumentative sequential context. The table is to be explicitly related to the experiential gap mentioned *earlier* and to the conclusion to *come*. All this is also related to the overall argumentative organisation of the book — the need to build on pupils' experiences, the importance of discussion, a high view of pop culture, the importance of pupils' own media creations, the desirability of a critical approach to public media producers, the importance of reorganising schools so as not to divide pupils, and the needs of the alienated, adolescent working class. The problem is to get from stuff such as tables to conclusions such as these, to get from a series of (mostly) responses and correlations to conclusions, suggestions and criticisms.

As has already been pointed out, the tables (at least as they are organised in the book) do not pre-date the argument. The expression 'to get from the tables to the conclusions' is then misleading. For the task is to organise the presentation of the tables *within* an argument about these things, in the case of Table 2 even titled and prefaced by them. The practical task is not relating a pile of dead factual statistics to some live implications for action, for the literary context of the table is already implicative. Nor, of course, do the authors have to get from this one table on teacher/pupils' different levels of television access to all the conclusions and implications. Nor do they have to move from table to implication *directly*. Nevertheless, there is an *impression* of shift. Now we are looking at some tables of alleged 'figures'; a moment later we are reading about experiential gaps. These are not disjunctive. We do not read them as we might a chapter change. They are different, but connected. We appear to *develop* naturally from one to another. And yet if we look at the table in isolation there is nothing there which *dictates* that the topical shift should occur in the direction in which it does. While the explanation is *consistent* with the table, it is only one explanation consistent with it. The feeling that it is a natural development of it, more than consistent with it, is a *managed* feeling. This is a general feature of social science texts.[19] Presented 'data', even initial argumentative statements, while they contain sleeping implications which a 'later' explanation or argumentative development may awake, are not directive. In taking up the explanation that he does the author is exercising an *option*. It may be a reasonable option, but it is an option. The explanation is 'one thing one might say about the table'. Rhetorically the author's task is to transform the explanation's optional into a natural status. He has to make it *the* consequence, *the* natural development of the table. That is the work he has to manage.

Chapter Three is a close analysis of how authors manage *natural development*. I do not wish to duplicate it here, but to make some simple remarks about the management of the transition in the case of the table and explanation of Table 2.

Above I write of the reader 'now' reading the table and 'now' reading the explanation as if one was done before the other. While this book is based on reading from start to finish, and while the importance of sequential position has constantly been emphasised, it has never been suggested that reading is a simple linear activity. Rather, as was pointed out in Chapter Two, it is a reflexive accomplishment in which early prose helps us to understand later prose and later prose helps us to 're-understand' the significance of earlier prose. There are plenty of textual equivalents of the conversational question *tag*[20] in which it may only be apparent that something *was* a question after it has been uttered. There are also equivalents in the proper reading of scientific arguments to the conversational 'Will you wait until I have finished before you criticise!' Sense is made both pro- and retrospectively in reading and this is *known* to and *expected* by readers and writers, at least intuitively. To manage an explanation so that it naturally develops from a table is not to manage each argumentative step so that it comes out of the previous step, the first step coming out of the table. It is to organise a chunk of explanation so that at a point several lines into the explanation, even at its end, the reader can see 'how it all fits'. The rhetorical power of this is enormous. The suspension of comprehension and criticism until the author has 'finished' means that things can never look the same again. Now the author has issued his argument and it colours all the evidence. It becomes a real effort to see the 'data' in other ways not influenced by the explanation.

In the case of Table 2, preceding pages have prepared us to find contrasts between teachers and pupils, and Table 1 has shown a difference between the newspapers which teachers read (buy? have access to?) and those read (bought? looked at?) by the 'general population'. Thus, argue the authors, the newspapers which are an 'integral part of the home environment of the majority of their working-class pupils'[21] are not read by most teachers. The discussion of newspaper reading stops immediately before Table 2 which comes, as it were, as a new paragraph on a new 'subject'. Given the title of the book, the preface and the existing juxtaposition of teachers and pupils, we can, however, see the television paragraph not as totally new but as *another* instance of teacher/pupil media discrepancy. The immediate explanation of the table emphasises this contrast, then something odd happens. The authors talk about what the table does *not* say! They assert that it conceals something. This is pure metaphor. There are obviously infinite things which any statement or table does not say. Moreover for it not to say them is not for it to 'conceal' them. What the concealment device allows the authors to do is to move naturally on to a something the table 'conceals' which *they* want to say, which is useful to their argument, and to move on *naturally*. The metaphor betrays itself since charges of concealment are usually made after one has found something![22]

The table has 'fixed' two categories, teachers and pupils, for contrast, but the contrast has not, I think, come off all that well. The sceptical reader might note that 83 per cent of teachers had the *same* level of access to television as their pupils. So the authors unfix the teacher category through the concealment metaphor, first on a school, then on an age-of-teacher basis. Once again, note that the table 'conceals' an infinite number of sub-categories. The authors have licence to choose these two, grammar school and young teachers. For these the figures are better, but still reveal that 69 per cent of those teachers with the least access to television had access to it compared to 98 per cent of pupils. The authors, of course, express it the other way round and as a fraction: 'Almost a third of the teachers under 25 had little or no contact with this part of their pupils' media experience'. But even so, it still is not the strongest sort of data. How then do they move from this to talk of experiential gap and complete that move in the three lines[23] starting 'However'?

a) 69 per cent of teachers with television sets is turned into 31 per cent of teachers without television.
b) 31 per cent is turned into 'nearly a third'.
c) 'Not having a television' is reformulated as 'having little or no

contact with this part of their pupils' media experience', i.e. the lack of television is displayed as *part* of a wider lack.

d) This new lack is dramatised by an ironic contrast with what 'could' have been. Suddenly the possibility that young teachers could have 'bridged the experiential gap' is introduced. As with the concealment metaphor, there are obviously lots of 'could have beens' and 'expecteds' which any table or result can be seen to 'disappoint'. The effect of bringing in one of these is to heighten the effect of the fraction by ironic contrast.

e) The 'in other respects' organises the 'lack' into the reverse of, or exclusion of, or barrier to 'bridging the gap'. 'In this respect' it says 'the teachers did not have the best chance of bridging the gap'. Lexically the 'gap' then comes into the text in a roundabout way. It comes from the dramatic contrast between an optional subdivision of one of the table's fixed categories and an arbitrary failed expectation. Even the subdivision is achieved by an arbitrary metaphor of concealment.

f) Thus a trivial statistical measurement is transformed by literary devices so that, whether we believe it or not, we find quite natural the authors' conclusion that young teachers will have *much* more difficulty establishing common ground with their pupils (my italics).

We can abstract some important elements of this:

1) 'Hard' numerical terms can be represented in many ways with differing argumentative implications.
2) In tables of relationships one can choose to emphasise contrast rather than similarity.
3) Style demands that the same word is not repeated too often. Under that umbrella, terms can be progressively recategorised from those of the table to those of the conclusion, while maintaining the 'illusion' that the same real world item is being referred to. Such recategorisation can proceed along a line of increasing generality. Since any social term is a potential part of several wholes, wider collectivities are easily implicated. Thus big conclusions can be implied out of small data.
4) Categories can be fixed and unfixed at the author's whim providing that he has enough in his data bank. If research has produced data on sex, class or age subdivisional variations, these can be introduced at times, as the argument develops.
5) Simple terms can do sophisticated argumentative work when set in sophisticated literary devices (e.g. irony, metaphor, etc.).

6) Absences, concealments and failed expectations are allowable topical development devices. Observations of X can be developed by noting that they contradict expectations, do *not* include a previously unmentioned Y, conceal a previously unmentioned Z, etc. Indeed there is a range of spatial expressions used elsewhere about observations, such as 'behind X', 'beyond X', 'at the root of X', and 'the deep or real implication of X', which permit the author to start talking about his preferred next topic, Y, yet do so as a natural development of X.[24]

7) More generally, we see the enormous licence which authors have to categorise items and relationships, to contrast, to emphasise, to measure, to generalise, to particularise, and in other ways *deploy* their words so that the reader moves naturally with them from table to conclusion.

### Diagrams

Much of what has been said about tables and other conventional data presentation forms applies to diagrams and need not be repeated. For not only do diagrams share these forms' interpolated character, structural effect and focusing effect, they even look like them! What is extremely striking about diagrams is their formal resemblance to statistical, graphical, chemical, electrical and cybernetic figures. There are diagrams which look like percentage tables:

A. **Fig. 3** Values transmitted by the pop media contrasted with those sponsored by the school

| Values sponsored by the school | Values transmitted by the pop media |
| --- | --- |
| work/production<br>preparing for the future<br>mind/intellect<br>self control | play/consumption<br>living in the present<br>body/emotion/feeling<br>physical and emotional expression |

From Figure 3 it is evident that the aspects of life which are emphasized by the pop media are those which are devalued or ignored within the schools. In the first place, the pop media prepare adolescents for their future role as consumers by introducing them to the notion of continuous and conspicuous consumption. Given that the continued viability of the present production system depends upon a high level of consumption, this aspect of the pop media could be considered as a logical complement to the rehearsal for work roles sponsored by the schools. Secondly, the pop media provide adolescents with a variety of ways of coming to terms with and expressing their developing emotional and physical capacities.

There are diagrams which look like graphs:

B. **Fig. 2** Diagrammatic representation of the relationship between the formal and informal school systems in the third year of a streamed school

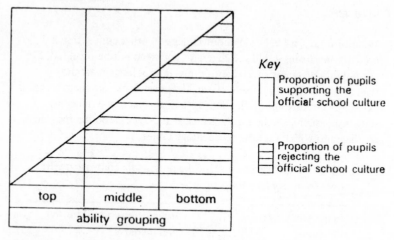

*Key*

Proportion of pupils supporting the 'official' school culture

Proportion of pupils rejecting the 'official' school culture

top   middle   bottom

ability grouping

There are diagrams which look like molecular structures:

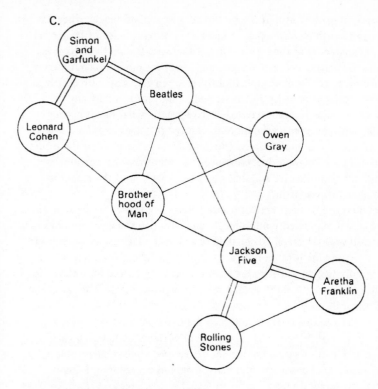

≡ close relationship (d < 43·0)

— some relationship (d < 48·0)

**Fig. 6** Diagrammatic representation of difference scores

And there are diagrams which look like printed circuits (though none in *Mass Media*). Diagrams also vary in complexity and abstraction. The names of their items can be the names of real institutions and actual people, or of means, types and abstractions. Some imply that they are imitating the spatial characteristics of the things they represent, e.g. scale: others do not. Some are very elliptical, leaving it to the reader to work out exactly how much they are saying, to what extent their message is allegorical and to what extent it is isomorphic. This variety of diagrams is, in a way, a nuisance in trying to present a short section on their rhetorical work. But, in another way, it is a most useful point to make. For it is precisely in their variety both of shapes, sizes, items, etc. and in their variable approximation to isomorphic devices or literary illustrations that the rhetorical potential of diagrams lies. In diagrams authors have open to them an enormous range of forms and types to deploy as they wish. First, if there are few methodological rules for writing prose arguments and fewer for presenting data, there are even fewer for diagrams. Bluntly, one can get away with a little in prose explanation, a lot in a table and an infinity in a diagram. Secondly, one does not have to declare exactly what one is getting away with. Diagrams even more than prose or tables have *layers* of suggestions and implications. The limiting factor is whether the reader will read the diagram. Is it worthwhile to reinforce one's argument with multi-implicative and unaccountable diagrams if the reader is not going to see them?

Of course, readers may also avoid chunks of prose, but very often prose is complicatedly interlocked, and although some prose books can be read very selectively using indices and other devices, judgement of their arguments is often not easy without fairly sustained reading. So it is with diagrams. They are forceful when interlocked with the prose, when the reader cannot make sense of the prose unless he looks at the diagram. But in two other ways the diagram may get looked at. First, there may be lots of them and they may, like tables, have a collective and serial effect. Secondly, and more important, some writers use diagrams as summaries and summaries are just what certain readers are interested in. Thus, certainly, many diagrams get ignored. Equally certainly many do not.

The first characteristic of Diagram A above is its strong formal resemblance to a statistical table, a percentage table. If it is compared with Table 2 discussed earlier, it can be seen that:

| 'Fig. 2' | replaces spatially and referentially | 'Table 2' |
| 'Values sponsored' | replaces | 'Teachers' |
| 'Values transmitted' | replaces | 'Pupils' |

and the contrast of values replaces the contrast of television access. Of course Fig. 3 is not a percentage table and there are differences between it and Table 2. Fig. 3 is essentially two contrasted lists. Why was it not arranged as such either in simple list form or after colons in the prose text? If we look at the lines which immediately follow Fig. 3, the answer is clear:

From Figure 3 it is evident that the aspects of life which are emphasized by the pop media are those which are devalued or ignored within the schools. In the first place, the pop media prepare adolescents for their future role as consumers by introducing them to the notion of continuous and conspicuous consumption. Given that the continued viability of the present production system depends upon a high level of consumption, this aspect of the pop media could be considered as a logical complement to the rehearsal for work roles sponsored by the schools. Secondly, the pop media provide adolescents with a variety of ways of coming to terms with and expressing their developing emotional and physical capacities.

First, the diagram allows the authors to treat the diagram in several ways as if it were data, for instance: they use it to start a new paragraph and to introduce the terms in the diagram from 'nowhere' (in data they would have to come from 'research' here they appear to be summaries of points argued separately during previous pages, but not in these formulations[25]): they use it to adopt the exegetical style and to derive the succeeding section as an explanation – 'From Fig. 3 it is evident . . .'

Secondly, the diagram helps the authors achieve the contrast they wish. And it helps them do so without them as it were signing their handiwork. The diagram seems to have items in it which contrast; indeed it is titled in that way. The authors accept responsibility for 'contrasting'. What they fail to point out is that they have arranged the items in the diagram so that they will contrast. They have not 'found' a contrast between bits of real world phenomena. They have constructed two lists and spatially arranged them so that they will contrast. The values are not so much sponsored by the school as by the authors, not so much transmitted by the pop media as by the authors.

It conveniently turns out that the school sponsors exactly the same number of values as the pop media – four. It is convenient that the items all contrast rather than are on continua or include each other. It is convenient that the authors do not have to show how such neat values are derived from observation and response. It is convenient that the categories of school and pop media are fixed and held as two homogeneities to be contrasted. It is convenient that the two lists are ordered so that diagonal relationships are not perceived, such as the mind/intellect involvement in play/consumption. It is convenient that the diagram can ignore the spatial and temporal contexts of values. Are there not times for work and times for play? Are there not places for work and places for play? Would it not be possible to erect just as plausible and just as contrived a diagram as this showing the complementary relationship of production and consumption, of leisure culture and school culture? Or again, could we not search out at least four ways in which pop media culture could be held to *resemble* school culture? I am sure some Marxist sociologist somewhere has suggested that pop culture and school both are sexist, non-revolutionary digressions from the real issues in society, emphasising the individual, excluding youth from real participation, alienations from traditional working-class culture. Such fancies are easy to manufacture. And that is what a diagram like this is — a fanciful manufacture in which the title announces a relationship that the author has organised to follow it. It is easy to solve the chess puzzle when you have arranged the pieces.

## Accounts

Authors make references, explicit and implicit, throughout their books to how they did their research. Some also have a section of the book in which such accounts are collected in a 'tale' of the research. This chapter concludes with some very brief comments about such tales. And the comments are brief because the issue of research tales is but a part of a far wider issue — that of accounts of the past. Grossly we can think of different ways of accounting the past: diaries, histories, reports, summaries and stories. And these each include sub-types. There are, for example, many different styles of reports. Conventionally these accounts are divided into factual and fictional varieties, the one reporting the real past, the other creating a past. But all these forms share the characteristic that they include techniques of item selection and arrangement. They are not controlled by past events, though they may have to recognise their audiences' existing knowledge of past events. They distil past events. Some of them are heavily ritualised. One thinks of schoolboy geometric reports with their 'Data, Required to Prove and Proof', or of the cumbersome passives and mimed actions of that style of physics reports in which 'the bunsen burner was taken'. In others the categories of the report and the ways in which they are sequentially combined reflect the organisational 'needs' of their recipients. One thinks perhaps of social work[26] or hospital reports.[27]

It is unclear, at least to me, exactly how research tales fit into these different forms. A proper consideration of them would, I suggest, compare and contrast them in a detailed way with these various forms in order to produce an analysis which, rejecting the fiction/fact dichotomy, would treat them as *constructions*. That is beyond this book, let alone this section.

These considerations can, however, shed a little light on Murdock and Phelps's tale of research. They use four appendices to tell the tale, totalling 42 pages. Appendix One describes how they chose the sort of approach they did. Appendix Two describes the 'planning and conduct of the research'. Appendix Three is 'Notes on specific measures', and Appendix Four contains supplementary tables. Appendix Two and the end of Appendix One are the focus of this section. A rough idea of Two's contents, too long to reproduce here, can be gained from its sub-headings:

> Appendix 2
>> The planning and conduct of the research
>> Stage I: The teachers' study
>>> Selecting the sample
>>>> Table 2.1 The ideal sample
>>>> Selecting education authorities
>>>> Selecting schools
>>> Administering the teachers' questionnaire
>>>> Table 2.2 The final sample for Stage I:
>>>> the teachers' questionnaire
>> Stage II: The pupils' questionnaire
>>> Selecting the schools
>>>> Fig. 2.2 Sample schools for Stage II
>>>> Fig. 2.3 Attitude and orientation scores of the ten study
>>>> schools. Note: The attitude and orientation scores intersect
>>>> at the overall means for all the schools in Stage I sample.
>>> Selecting the pupils
>>> Administering the questionnaire
>>>> Table 2.3 Number of pupils who participated in Stage II
>> Stage III: Interviewing the selected pupils
>>> Table 2.4 Basic groupings: pop involvement/school
>>> commitment

And a similarly rough idea of the style can be gained from this excerpt from Appendix One:

Our research design (illustrated in Fig. 1.1) attempted to put into practice the theoretical perspective offered by Mills' idea of the sociological imagination.

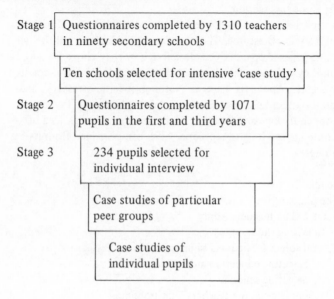

Fig. 1.1 Research design

At Stage 1 we started with a general survey of teachers in ninety widely different sorts of secondary schools in various parts of England, concentrating particularly on their attitudes towards the mass media and their approach to using media material in the classroom. On the basis of the questionnaire returns we selected ten schools which represented the diversity of attitudes and approaches, for more intensive study at Stage 2. These case studies were intended to provide concrete illustrations of the general structures revealed by the survey. Within these ten schools we gave a self-completion questionnaire to pupils in the first and third years, and on the basis of these returns we selected a number of pupils for intensive personal interview at Stage 3. Again the interview material was seen as a way of building up a series of case studies of particular groups of pupils and of individual pupils who occupied specific positions within the school's social structures as revealed by the questionnaire. We further supplemented the survey data with a short test designed to elicit pupils' pop music preferences, conducted with classroom groups. We also took every opportunity to talk to the staff and to observe the patterns of social relationships within the schools.*

*A full account of how each stage of the research was planned and conducted may be found in Appendix 2.

The first problem with this tale of research is about its recipient. For whom is it intended? And that is related to another, 'Who will read it?'. And that is related to another, 'How will they read it?'. It is these questions which are a little difficult to answer. We might start by speculating that, to a degree, the tale is ritualistic. It is there because it is usual to give an account in case anyone wishes to read it, to show that there is a tale to account, to show that one can tell it, whether anyone actually reads it or not. Then there are those who might treat the tale as a check list. They can approach it with a shopping list of methodological enquiries:

How did the authors sample? . . . . . . . . . . . . . . . . . . . . . . I see
What was the return rate? . . . . . . . . . . . . . . . . . . . . . . . . I see
How long were the interviews? . . . . . . . . . . . . . . . . . . . . I see
What were the stages? . . . . . . . . . . . . . . . . . . . . . . . . . . I see
Were rural areas included? . . . . . . . . . . . . . . . . . . . . . . I see

But not all readers will do this and those who do will find that the tale is not just a check list, though it is headed so as to help someone complete one. It is in prose and does more than give sampling facts and other information. It *explains*, *justifies*, and excuses the researchers' actions:

The final sample . . . does not differ markedly from our ideal except for the lack of single sex comprehensives. Since these are in any case relatively rare, no attempt was made to compensate for this deficiency.[28]

It shows the researcher as thorough and thoughtful and considerate to the teachers:

The questionnaires were delivered to all schools by the research staff who, wherever possible, spoke to the teachers about the questionnaire and the research in general.[29]

It shows them encountering difficulties usually caused by others:

Unfortunately, Woodfields dropped out . . . The headmaster had taken up another appointment without warning us of his departure and his successor could not be persuaded to let us continue our work.[30]

Obviously, if it is possible that a large proportion of readers do not read these tales carefully it would be silly to exaggerate their rhetorical impact, especially the impact of individual sentences. But if we flick through the pages, glancing at the headings, reading the odd paragraph, it is possible to get a rhetorical impression. And that impression is a *generalisation* of the check-list approach. It is that, given their problems and resources, these authors' researches are *in order*. They have worked hard, overcome difficulties, adjusted to setbacks, been considerate to their subjects, observed the rule book of methods, and so on. The account boosts the authors' credibility *generally*. For, unlike the check-list reader, the reader who glosses the appendix is interested in general questions. He does not so much want to check this research device as the general bona fides of the authors. He does not read the few research details that catch his eye and rush back home to check them. He reads them generatively. If he reads that the authors sampled carefully, he can see that they were careful about *other* 'things like that'. Before we find this notion of generative reading purely speculative, it is as well to look at the text.

Recalling the earlier discussion, the tale is not like a diary nor like a history (at least an old fashioned one with dates). It does contain odd temporal references, but one could not, for instance, reconstruct a history of the research from the tale. Most obviously a large number of its statements are not about unit events, about individual things which individual people do, but are summary remarks. Some are obviously repeated actions: 'Of the 234 pupils who were interviewed'.[31] Some are the implied results of sustained action or deliberation: 'Consequently, at the end of the preliminary stage, we arrived at the ideal sample'.[32] Some are actions collecting a *series* of tasks: 'Pupil replies were noted by the interviewer on a schedule'.[33] These items in the tale are repetitions, serials, lines of developments, stages, processes, aggregates, and so on. Moreover they are arranged to interlock with each other. The order is not 'we did this on Monday, then this on Tuesday', but it is 'logical'. See for example the research design figure above. The effect of all this is to generate. The reader who glosses bits has his attention directed to overall schemes, previous actions, cumulations, etc.

A second aspect of the way the authors construct their tale is their avoidance of untidiness. There are no loose ends. They do not tell us of the data they could not make sense of. There are no results which do not fit into stages. There are no indications of what 'I' did and what 'he' did, the research staff do everything unanimously. Obviously there is not room in an account to talk of the millions of actions that occurred over the four years of research. Obviously events have to be organised into chunks of actions. They have to be put under headings. But, equally obviously, the chunks and headings used here capture none of the practicality, complexity and ad hocery of daily life. Take the *Mass Media* account and see how far one can derive from it a research programme that actual people in actual circumstances on actual days could do. It will be found that it really does not go into *how* things are done at all. It merely gives them names, names which suggest qualities and capabilities in the authors. Or another way to look at this difficult issue is to ask what sort of model of researcher the *Mass Media* authors imply in their account. In the excerpted piece the model researcher

'*starts* with a general survey'

'*concentrates* on attitudes'  } my italics

'*selects* on the basis of questionnaire returns'

And in Appendix Two these are broken down into component actions, such as: 'A small number of schools declined to help us and these were *replaced* by similar schools from the same area'[34] (my italics). If we ask 'Where was the researcher when he 'replaced' them? When did he 'replace' them?' we see that replacement is not so much a thing one does but the *result* of mundane activities such as telephoning Mr X, thinking about possible replacements, etc. Even things superficially initiative, such as 'starting with a general survey', describe the result of mundane action. And results such as these are seeable as the proper business of research. What happens when they are used as headings for the mundane actions of researchers is that they take the myriad actions and interactions of researchers, their musings, their talk, their wishes, intentions and resolutions, and replace them with a term which conflates intention, action, interaction and reflection in 'result'.

Perhaps the whole matter can be put more simply than this. The account of research is not meant to replace the research itself. It is not research into the research. The *Mass Media* authors obviously think it worthwhile in analysing the social phenomena of mass media to use social science techniques and to research for some time. But their own activities over four years are social phenomena. Since they use no such techniques to analyse it, we must treat their account more as a lay account, as the account of any educated person writing about his work over the last four years. As such it is different from the rest of their book. Their research expertise is in mass media in secondary schools, not in writing about research. When it comes to writing a research account they will do pretty much what anyone would do when called on to write up his work. They will give an account which seeks to unify the last four years as a scheme with sub-schemes. In that structure they will distil and collect events in terms of their results for the sub and overall schemes. They are concerned to display the rational order of their activities, not with the description of the activities themselves. And that concern will lead them to see and write about those activities in a certain way. That way need have no element of deceit about it. Their account will probably be, and I am sure in the case of *Mass Media*, is *true*. But it will also be a metaphor. It will tell the past in a pattern, a pattern designed to demonstrate certain aspects.

From the point of view of rhetoric, the research tale is of interest not so much for particular devices, such as capacity to generate a bona fide picture of the researcher for the glossing reader, as for its reinforcement of a certain high view of research. For there is always the danger that the reader may think the pattern that the account brings to the research is the pattern *of* the research; that the rational scheme in which the tale of the research is cast is the rational day-to-day action of researchers. Readers should not treat *a* quite truthful way of accounting research as a reliable guide for *the* definitive picture of the researcher.

## Notes

1. But see later in this section where this definition is discarded.
2. Also see later where this definition is discarded.
3. I.A. Richards, *The Philosophy of Rhetoric*, (Oxford University Press, New York, 1965), p. 5.
4. G. Murdock and G. Phelps, Schools Council Research Study, *Mass Media and the Secondary School* (Macmillan, London, 1973).
5. Schools Council/Nuffield Humanities Project, *The Humanities Project: An Introduction*, (Heinemann, London, 1970).
6. Schools Council, *Religious Education in Primary Schools: Discovering an Approach*, (Macmillan, London, 1977).
7. Schools Council, Health Education Project 9-13, Introductory Booklet, (Nelson, London, 1977).
8. 'Our research was primarily oriented . . . towards contributing information to a crucial ongoing debate about public educational policy − the raising of the

school leaving age and the shape of the future secondary curriculum'. Schools Council, *Mass Media*, p. 159.

9. I think *all* these have explanations but in some cases the relationship between prose and interpolation is implicit.

10. Schools Council, *Mass Media*, Appendices 1-4.

11. *Mass Media*'s conventional interpolations are mostly tabular. There are others linked with Semantic Differential Schedules and Factor Analysis. I do not consider these.

12. H. Garfinkel and H. Sacks, 'On the formal structures of Practical Actions', in J.C. McKinney and E.A. Tivyakian (eds), *Theoretical Sociology: Perspectives and Development*, (Appleton-Century-Crofts, New York, 1970).

13. D. Huff, *How to Lie with Statistics*, (Penguin, London, 1973).

14. A.V. Cicourel, *Method and Measurement in Sociology*, (Free Press, New York, 1964).

15. Schools Council, *Mass Media*, Appendix 1, pp. 156-60.

16. D.C. Anderson, 'Stories and Argument', *Pragmatics Microfiche*, PM 3.1.E, 1978.

17. Schools Council, *Mass Media*, p. 141.

18. E.A. Schegloff, 'Notes on a Conversational: Formulating Place', in D. Sudnow (ed.), *Studies in Social Interaction*, (Free Press, New York, 1972).

19. D.C. Anderson, 'Literary and Rhetorical Features in the Local Organisation of Sociological Arguments', Ph.D. thesis, Brunel University (1977).

20. H. Sacks, Lectures, UCLA and Irvine (some of the lectures are published in *Pragmatics Microfiche*).

21. Schools Council, *Mass Media*, p. 5.

22. D.C. Anderson and W.W. Sharrock, 'On the Usefulness of Illustrated Ideology as a Method for Analysing the Media', to appear in M. Cain and J. Finch, (eds), *From Epistemology to Methods*.

23. I except two lines which I read as digression from the argument.

24. Anderson and Sharrock, 'Irony as a Methodological Convenience', in E.L. Wright (ed.), *Irony*, (Harvester, in press).

25. After re-reading the chapter several times I am still unclear how to represent the origins of these terms.

26. D.C. Anderson, 'Social Work Reports and the Grammar of Organisational Reaction', *Analytic Sociology*, Vol. 1, No. 3 (1978).

27. H. Garfinkel, Studies in Ethnomethodology, (Prentice Hall, Englewood Cliffs, 1967).

28. The Schools Council, *Mass Media*, p. 166.

29. Ibid.

30. Ibid., p. 171.

31. Ibid.

32. Ibid., p. 165.

33. Ibid., p. 171.

34. Ibid., p. 166.

The extract on pp. 120-1 is reproduced by permission from *Mass Media and the Secondary School,* by Graham Murdock and Guy Phelps (Schools Council Research Studies, Macmillan Education, 1973).

# 5 BORROWING VERISIMILITUDE

## Introduction

There are times, as we read through an academic text, when we feel the author is himself arguing his case and, as it were, arguing it for the first time. At other moments we are aware that the author is re-presenting work which he has done elsewhere and at another time. Then there are passages in which the author justifies his case not by current argument nor his own previous argument but by someone else's argument. He is borrowing justification. In Chapter Two we saw that borrowed justifications may be introduced into a text by citation, by exemplification, by quotation and by several other marginal devices with which the author can partially disclaim authorship of a statement. We also saw that there are good reasons to be especially alert to borrowing practices in a text of a discipline such as education which is parasitic on other disciplines. And we characterised borrowing as consisting of a rhetorical transfer in which the borrowed fact, concept, perspective or whatever, is deprived of its 'original' textual and organisational context and surrounded by a new textual and organisational context worked up by the 'new' author. Let us refer to these two processes as 'cutting out' and 'working up'.[1]

Chapter Two did not explore, however, the range of items which may be borrowed. Obviously that range of items will include 'facts': authors may use, for example, a citation to introduce 'facts' established in some other text. In this case the other text may have justified the 'fact' by hypothesis testing or some other scientific convention. Authors also borrow concepts or perspectives. And in this case the original text will have justified these by proving them useful or by establishing that they are conventional (i.e. widely used within the original discipline). Authors may also borrow what I shall call 'verisimilitude'. By this I mean an item which makes the reader feel close to the subject or which brings the subject close to experiences in the reader's life. Some people speak of texts 'ringing true', of them being 'lifelike' or 'realistic', of them 'telling it like it is'.

All three types of item are conventionally regarded as points in favour of a text and certainly it helps us to accept and believe the text if we find it not only factual, evidenced, proven, tested, etc.; not only useful in reconsidering a problem or area but familiar, touching our interests and experiences and recognisable. Convention also assigns

126

these good qualities of texts to different types of texts. Thus it is the
job of scientific, academic texts to convince their readers by proof,
evidence, tests and facts. It is the job of teaching texts to help readers
see things in new and useful ways. And it is the job of literature, of
'fiction', to touch our experience, to involve the reader's sentiments
and his 'world' in the 'world' of the text. In practice, within
education and the social sciences, it is immediately obvious that one
and the same text may aim to be scientifically convincing and
educationally useful. The cult of perspectives is not confined to
classrooms and teaching books but is well entrenched in 'scientific' and
academic books. In particular the assault on positivism in the sixties[2]
has led many to doubt whether facts and proofs are as accessible in
matters such as education as was once thought[3] and, consequently, to
merge, or more often confuse, ideas of truth and use.[4] The essence of
that cult is to take a familiar subject and show that by looking at it
from a different vantage point one can see it differently: 'take as
central a Marxist perspective, take as central the concept of decision-
making,[5] take as central the importance of democratic discussion,[6]
take as central Piagetian theories of child development,[7] take as central
the link between moral choice and interpersonal interaction,[8] take as
central the concept of social class,[9] then you will be able to see your
school, your health education, your humanities teaching, your
religious education, your moral education and your treatment of the
media in a new light'. The burden on the author is not to 'prove'
anything but to show just how 'new' this light is, just how many
familiar activities it illuminates, just how many teachers felt it 'helpful',
just how many pupils responded to it, etc. And in order to claim these
'benefits' for the perspective, the author has to demonstrate some
consistency of activity and perspective. He has to show the reader how
these teacher or pupil activities may be seen as examples of the
perspective in action. The bulk of the author's work and of the pages
of his text are spent in showing the usefulness, productivity,
fascination and potential of his perspective in action (a topic treated
in the next chapter, 'Achieving Practicality'). The perspective itself
is quasi-axiomatic. And one rhetorical function of borrowing is to
avoid the business of justifying the perspective initially.[10] Whether the
perspective is a fairly precise one such as 'self-concept' or a vaguer one
such as 'discovery', 'community', or 'democracy', the author will wish
to steer his reader away from the 'awkward question' which is not 'Is
your perspective useful?' but 'Why should I adopt it rather than any
other?' The conventional academic way to justify one-approach-rather-

than-another is to do a thorough analysis of the competition in a
literature search, and an equally thorough analysis of the existing
practices which the innovation, the new approach is designed to change.
(By 'thorough' I mean an analysis which matches the depth, scope,
and expense of the innovation's intended field of application).
Borrowing helps the author avoid these tasks. It permits the poorly
financed, over-committed curricular researcher, harrassed by teachers
who want this feature, funders who want that feature and colleagues
who want the other feature, to jump the initial work of research, get
down to 'the useful bit' and justify his funds. That jump not only
reduces his work load; it removes from him the most dangerous
criticism which could be made of his work. For the consequences of an
anarchic relativism which invites readers to look at things 'this way' is
to produce an infinite stream of possible perspectives[11] and the
existence of a multitude of other actual or possible perspectives is a
severe threat to the author. It threatens him with a change of argument.
If these other perspectives are admitted, his work becomes justifying-
my-approach-rather-than-theirs, instead of simply showing how my
approach can be productive. Careful borrowing of facts and
perspectives will allow an author to cut out the controversy which
surrounds so many 'facts' in their parent disciplines and to avoid
detailed discussion of the relative merits of the perspective borrowed.
The argument can then be started from that point on. Thus borrowing
should be seen as one of many devices which control controversy.
In presentation of research, as in doing it, it is important not to ask
too many questions or none may be answered. In research only so
many variables can be considered. In argument only some questions
may be asked. Aspects of books such as the division of topics into
chapters and paragraphs,[12] and the use of titles[13] which focus attention
on this and not the many other questions about the subject to be dealt
with, as well as the use of borrowing to delineate what this book deals
with and what it does not (but others do), are all part of this work of
controversy control.

## Verisimilitude

If in practice the borrowing of perspective is not confined to pedagogic
books, nor is the achievement of verisimilitude confined to works of
fiction. In many academic texts we find a concern with verisimilitude
and with the reader's empathy. In academic texts we find poetic,

dramatic and neo-classical rhetorical devices employed in the service of verisimilitude and reader empathy. In this chapter I focus on the achievement of verisimilitude as one effect of *borrowing*.

It is important first to realise just how much it will profit the author if he can achieve verisimilitude. Most obviously the book which 'rings true' to the reader's experience and excites his emotions will be read more enjoyably. That enjoyment may well affect the relationship between reader and writer. Not only may it dispose the reader to a generally benign view of the author, it may also lead him to find that the author is 'one of us', i.e. perhaps someone with common professional experiences. It may, depending on how it is done, also show the author as related in some way, of which the reader approves, to his subject. In curricular texts, for example, one can write, so as to show one 'really cares about kids' or that one is sympathetic to teachers' problems. And if the reader also 'really cares about kids' and is a teacher this reciprocity of emotions will be a bond between reader and writer which may well influence the criticism the former will make of the latter. If such bonds can be established they can lead to the reader reading in a different and very generative way. Garfinkel talks about statements having 'Et Cetera' clauses.[14] By this he means that such expressions as instructions are not exhaustive but need to be read with a knowledge of circumstances to and in which they might apply. They need to be completed for this or that practical circumstance. The reader who empathises with a writer can not only understand what the writer means but can extend it. Most crucially, he can find extra instances of it. To the author's description of *a* pupil, *a* classroom, or *a* lesson the teacher (or ex-) teacher reader can add others like it. The author can be read elliptically as providing simply the start of arguments, the first few of a list of examples, or evidences to which the reader will append more from his experience. There is then a sense in which not only the author may get the reader to complete the author's argument for himself: but because the reader completes it, the argument becomes the reader's. It is 'his' argument. And he identifies with it.

All this suggests that verisimilitude might be a useful thing for the author to achieve in addition to 'scientific' credibility. It is a good thing if, in addition to offering good evidence and logical argument, the author can make his study appealing, interesting and lifelike. However, verisimilitude may go further than this and *substitute* for evidence and argument. This may occur in two inter-connected circumstances. In the last fifteen years methodologists in the mainstream of social science and more latterly in education and curriculum studies have asked what sort of methodology is necessary to study social as distinct from natural phenomena. Pointing out that in the study of the former the student is a member of his topic and has inter-subjective access to it, and that the objects of social research, unlike the objects of natural scientific research, have themselves views about themselves, such methodologists have raised a variety of problems and solutions.[15] Some stress the importance of natural over experimental methods; some talk of being 'faithful to the phenomena'; some stress the importance of validity over reliability; others wish to study the social world from the 'inside', from 'the actor's point of view'. In practice these ideas result in closer observation of fewer people; more talking with the objects of study in longer and fewer interviews; participation in the circumstances of the people studied; methodic attention to the way people reveal their own understandings of their interactional circumstances through utterance response;[16] more use of spontaneous talk; and more serious attention to the records people make of their own lives.[17] The advantages and disadvantages of these views and methods are not at issue here. What is clear is that, *to an extent*, a style of research which identifies or comes close to identifying method with verisimilitude is now *legitimate*. In the subjects most responsible for pioneering these methods such as cognitive anthropology and (American) sociology, these 'qualitative methods' can be each identified, linked with certain well-known names, certain theories, certain studies and certain advantages and disadvantages. Another way to look at these advantages and disadvantages is to say that each method *releases* the researcher from some tasks which other methods would have him do, but gives him another set of tasks. These others are, arguably, equally demanding. Thus, to study a school by participant observation *may* release one from the work of sampling and questionnaire design, but it imposes a training in observation, problems of access, work in recording, etc. To work with audio and video tapes may release one from observation and access but imposes a training in aspects of linguistics, possibly hours of transcription, a technical expertise (in the case of some video recording) and considerable analytic work. When these methods are generally imported into curriculum work, when they are borrowed, there is a tendency to borrow the idea and justification and to leave behind the problems and detailed work. For example, much of the English research in curriculum has clearly abandoned a quantitative method. Some of it explicitly claims a qualitative stance in the term 'illuminative'[18] for instance. Yet the well-known problems of the different styles of qualitative work are left behind when they are borrowed, and in many cases so are their disciplines. I know of *no rigorous* English curricular work in a symbolic-interactionalist, a cognitive anthropological, a phenomenological or an ethnomethodological style.[19]

The second and interrelated circumstance is that many *teachers* feel that some areas of their work are not amenable to quantitative analysis. Most obviously this is so in the field of evaluation where, in varying ways and to varying degrees, it is said that there are some important things which one just cannot evaluate in terms of percentages, rates and tables. More generally it is felt that teaching is concerned with 'individual children' not with statistics.[20] Thus, both in academic and in everyday readers an author may find a response which does not seek proof in science and may find it in verisimilitude. For the author to adopt an approach which is loosely qualitative may then absolve him from the rigours of quantitative research without imposing those of the specific methods of qualitative research and yet permit him to retain the possibility, even the increased possibility, of persuading his readers.

If an author opts for this policy it *does* impose on him the stylistic work of achieving verisimilitude. If he has renounced the work involved in both quantitative and qualitative methods he *will* have to work hard stylistically to make his book 'ring true'. This hard work will employ lots of devices, but two which are common are anecdotes and quotations from pupils and teachers. The anecdote is of course enshrined, in an extended form, in methodology as the *case study* but also exists in much shorter, less explicit and less formalised formats. The remainder of this chapter looks at the borrowing of facts, perspectives and verisimilitudes through quotations used in the Schools Council Project, *Religious Education in Primary Schools: Discovering an Approach*.[21] (Henceforth *Religious Education*).

### Quotations

Quotations, mostly of children talking, the space between quotations and the body of the text, and other inserts such as diagrams take up a lot of space in *Religious Education* (a matter we return to later). Chapter Three, entitled 'Children and Religious Education', structurally involves quotations in its argument as follows:

1. 'If it is to be relevant, religious education must take account of the ways in which children think and learn . . . Do (the ways children

think and feel about religion) change as children grow?'

2. Children make sense of religion developmentally. Adults do not have full access to these senses *'the best they can do is gather clues and gain insights*. Researchers . . . have to gather their information and present their findings in a way that is not distorted by their adult perspective.' (My italics)

3. Piaget's work has greatly influenced this research. (Piaget is then summarised, (15 lines), and the three stages of development intuitive, concrete and abstract outlined (22 lines)).

4. Accounts of further research by Goldman on religious education variations of the 'stages' and of research into children's 'feelings', the 'inner world of the child'.

5. 1-4 consists of the authors' account of other people's work, other researchers. They follow this by pointing out that teachers not only draw on research but their own 'knowledge and observation of children'. Then starts the main and longest part of the chapter consisting of quotes from children linked by explanations from the authors which we are, I think, meant to read as showing how the concepts and ideas of the borrowed researchers fit the thoughts and feelings of the children as revealed in the quotes. On the basis of this fit, this illumination of the quotes by the researches and vice versa, the authors make suggestions for the teaching of religious education. The quotes are dealt with in the three 'stage' blocks, age six — intuitive, age eight — concrete, age eleven — abstract. The start of the middle block reads:

*An eight-year-old*

Thinking and learning

A clue to the thinking and learning of an eight-year-old is his interest in the 'concrete', that is, actual situations, sensory experiences, tangible objects and verifiable facts.

He is excited by a world over which he has increasing physical and mental power. For example, he internalises the tangible world into his thoughts with so much more ease than when he was six, that he seems to revel in his prowess. He collects and arranges facts as avidly as he collects and arranges stamps, cigarette cards and marbles.

Because of this emphasis on the concrete, learning by doing, discovering for himself, manipulating and constructing are important to him and his ability to read and write increases the scope of his discovery.

His interest in things, facts and activities make an eight-year-old ready for more systematic learning about the religions he sees in the world around him: buildings, customs and the things people do.

### The importance of language

His thinking is limited in that it centres on the concrete as can be seen by the way he handles religious ideas.

*I think God is a giant man that can hold the world.* Peter

*Sometimes everybody makes a mistake; surely everybody makes a mistake sometimes. I make mistakes. I think God makes mistakes sometimes like me; God makes mistakes like babies with no arms.*

His spontaneous talk shows his continuing interest in how things began, how they work and why they are as they are.

*My mystery is about speech. It is a mystery to you but it is not to the one who is going to speak.* Anthony

*My mystery is why our mummy has babies now and again.* Nicholas

*I have never seen a jungle in my life. I can see pictures of a jungle but it is a mystery to me what a jungle is really like.* Colin

He is often fascinated by language, especially as he becomes more proficient in its use and enjoys jokes, riddles and puns.

Giving the eight-year-old the opportunity to question and discuss, especially as he explores the dimension of wonder and mystery in his experience, is an important part of religious education.

Although I give this account for readers who do not have access to *Religious Education* and yet who wish to see how quotes fit in to the chapter context, it does show how central the quotes are for the chapter. Although the authors suggest the quotes 'illustrate'[22] the children's thinking, they clearly do not mean 'illustrate' in the sense that the quotes are ornamental. The quotes are abundant and central to the authors' argument. Indeed they repeatedly treat the quotes as giving access to thoughts:

'His spontaneous talk shows his continuing interest in how things began' (from the above excerpt).
'His spontaneous talk shows he is concerned . . . about the mysteries of life'[23]
and

'an eleven-year-old's talk and writing show him reaching out to grasp abstract ideas . . .'[24]

To say that the quotes are central to the authors' argument is not to say that the authors treat them as research. Indeed, these particular authors are rather reticent about the status of the quotes. Are they the 'clues' referred to at the start of the chapter? Is 'show' to be read subjunctively as saying 'could be regarded as pointing to'? Is their assertion that the quotes are of *typical* six, eight and eleven-year-olds to be taken strongly or softly? If the quotes are from a 'bank' of quotes which the authors possess, a bank regarded as part of the authors' research of which 'only a small part could be included in the book',[25] are they related to that bank methodically or are they merely the most suitable for the book? Again the issue is not whether such reticence is naughty. The issue is that there are now very large numbers of quasi-research[26] books on the market, books whose mixed and reticent methodological status leaves the critic uncertain not only of how to treat the book in general but of how to scrutinise aspects, such as quotations, in particular. Making allowance for such uncertainty, some comments may be made about these particular quotes and the use made of them, comments which raise some general issues about quoting in curriculum texts.

**Cutting Out**

The authors attach names to the quotes. The quotes are then attributed to Peter, Anthony, Nicholas, etc. The names are Christian names. Why should they do such a thing? First I can note that the practice makes me feel that the authors have a certain disposition to the children. Unlike a categorisation of the children 'a boy in an inner-city school in Belfast' or a research designation 'Child C', the use of the Christian name puts the researchers into the group of people who might use a Christian name, teachers, parents, neighbours, etc. The researchers are not cold-blooded statisticians but have a real interest in the individual children. Whether this feeling of mine is well founded or not, for me the use of Christian names is part of the achievement of verisimilitude. What it is certainly not is an accurate allocation of the quote. Some of the quotes are claimed to be from 'spontaneous talk' but they resemble nothing of the kind. Chapter Six has some transcript of talk and it does not look like these quotes.[27] They have quite obviously had accent, stress, hesitation, aspiration, elongation, repetition and all the other hall marks of natural talk removed. They have had their conversational context obliterated. We do not know where or when they were said. We do not know what talk they were a development of, what other persons' talk they were responses to. In short they are not the talk of Peter, Anthony and Nicholas but of the authors. Nor are they typical talk. The authors have either chosen or amended the quotes so as to have none of those in which non-lexical noises, sub-audible mutterings and untranscribable overlaps and other phenomena are present. It becomes clear that, in saying that the talk is typical, the authors refer only to what we may call its topical coverage. What they mean is that they have heard other children talking of the same matters as these children, showing the same interests and feelings.

None of this need matter. There are a number of ways in the social sciences to treat talk. There are structuralist approaches,[28] content analysis approaches,[29] conversational analytic approaches[30] and story grammar approaches,[31] to name but a few. In this particular context there are also methods pioneered in biblical exegesis which, while concerned with texts rather than talk, also demonstrate a sophisticated generaliseable emphasis on sequential and other types of context. There is also a whole tradition of rhetoric. Some of these methods might insist on detailed transcript, others might not. Some might emphasise social context, others might not. Some might be interested in the form of the quote, others not.

But the authors do not use *any* of these methods or if they do, they do not show their 'working'. They do not even admit they exist. And we must conclude that whether or not the authors claim the quotes as evidence (and that is unsure) these quotes are certainly not evidence. The interesting question is 'What are they?' And that question can be refined by looking to see what the authors do with the quotes, especially how they work up a new context for them.

### Working Up

The authors work up the quotes in two ways. First, they treat the quote itself, by, for example, adding the Christian name, and conventionalising the prose. Secondly, they organise a receiving context for the quote. Our lack of access to the original makes analysis of the first aspect difficult. But we might hazard a few speculations. The essence of the author's strategy is to move from a consideration of the 'pupils'' talk to one of their concepts and feelings. Both by tidying and conventionalising the talk and by only including the most conventional of quotes, they omit such talk as might make us question whether or not the children have *any* concept! The quotes they give are to show the reader several different sorts of coherent inner world. They are designed to show three sorts of thinking. The risk with a lot of what children say is, bluntly, that it does not fit into these sorts. Some of it does not even suggest to the adult any known thinking. Once again I refer the reader to the transcripts in Chapter Six. Children then say things which *can* be seen (by adults) to be thoughtful and others which cannot. Some of the thoughtful things they say can be allocated to one of the three stages. Some cannot. This is of no consequence in itself as no reasonable person expects a theory or categorisation scheme to handle all phenomena. But in this chapter the authors are arguing for the *relevance* of the theory and scheme for children as revealed by their talk and to do so they arrange the talk in such a way that the theory and schemes potentially fit. Their altering of children's talk is not only alteration involving the loss of original context, but alteration towards sentential and other forms which suggest coherence and intelligibility.

Or another way of looking at this is to take the commonplace observation that, at first sight, accurately transcripted talk makes people appear stupid.[32] They are found to be Umming, Aahing, repeating, not finishing sentences, etc. The converse of this is that a first sight of a tidied conventionalised transcript makes people appear clever. By tidying their transcripts as they do, the authors upgrade their children. This not only fits nicely with the Piagetian scheme and helps their argument for the relevance of that scheme, it also shows them 'taking children seriously', 'not considering them as deficient adults' and all those sorts of things likely to be approved of by those who 'work with kids'.

This work of up-grading the child's world is also tackled by the explanatory sections linking the quotes. Before or after every quote we are told what the child is doing. In the excerpted section we find children being 'interested in how things began, how they work and why they are as they are'. In other sections, children are 'concerned about the mysteries of life',[33] show 'sensitivity to the experiences of others'[34] and are undergoing 'idealism'.[35] Now obviously it is the job of the authors to do something *general* with these quotes. The reader is not interested in the individual children for themselves, but in how their thinking and feeling can help him understand other children, perhaps his own pupils. Therefore, quite reasonably, we expect the authors to be commenting on the quotes in order to produce theories, hypotheses, and hunches. We expect generalisation. And that generalisation we expect to occur with regard to the children and their thoughts. We wish to move from Nicholas to eight-year-olds in general and from 'mystery of speech' to a general characterisation as being interested in how things began, etc. One by-product of showing how one person's statement can be generalised is that the person himself may get credited with the generalisation. Many readers will have experienced the sensation of feeling more forgiving towards a person's offensive action when they have heard another person's explanation of it. Or another example,[36] theories about the structure of language do not imply that children learn language that way. For always with attempts to theorise about the actions of humans there is the risk of equating the analyst's explanation and the subject's intention or action. It has been particularly noticed in ethnographic studies that a result of close study of someone's world is to reveal that world as altogether more complex and rich than was previously thought. That is one error due to a methodological side effect of close analysis. Another error, a compound error, is to continue and find that the occupant of this world must indeed be clever to manage it. Certain sorts of analysis can, then, finish up crediting actors with analyst's thoughts and, since analyst's thoughts are professional thoughts, these analyses can portray the actor very favourably. The danger of these two errors is particularly likely with children. The excerpt furnishes a good example:

> His spontaneous talk shows his continuing interest in how things began, how they work and why they are as they are.
> My mystery is about speech. It is a mystery to you but it is not to the one who is going to speak. Anthony

In this particular section 'His' may refer to the 'eight-year-old' introduced above. But quite clearly in two other places the authors attribute 'the dimension of wonder' and the 'dimension of mystery'[37] to the child. Whether children all have a dimension of wonder or whether some simply express wonder at some things is not the point at issue. The point is not about developmental psychology. It is that in crediting children with such adult and analyst-derived generalisations as a 'dimension of wonder' on the basis of illustrative quotes about *a* wondering statement, is to upgrade an utterance into a capacity. And this is a general orientation in this chapter. The authors use quotes to point to general analytic concepts and in their move (a perfectly reasonable move from example to principle, from incident to theory) they involve the child. Once again the sentimental effect of their work is to draw themselves close to the child.

Argumentatively there is also an effect. The general conflation of statement and capacity, and individual child and the typical child is to obscure the real difficulties which confront the teacher using these arguments. For the teacher finds herself dealing with children making utterances in particular settings. Her job is to respond to the particular utterance of the particular child in the particular setting. Her work is practical reasoning, reasoning in a restricted, particularised setting. And the reasoning she is to respond to in the child is practical and situated as well. To use the sort of remarks made in this chapter in the . classroom involves the teacher in an operation to see particularised interactions as instances of generalised forms, an operation similar to the seeing of quotes as examples of argumentative points. Neither of these operations which Cicourel calls those of 'fit' are addressed by the authors.[38]

Obviously, teachers find generalised strategies useful as well and Chapter Three may be very useful to teachers as a general guide. But in my Chapter Six I shall argue that most curriculum projects are not practical if we mean by practical that they have a sustained and detailed interest in the settings in which actions are enacted. Certainly this chapter of *Religious Education* is concerned with the theoretic and not with the practical. However, the quotes which are portrayed as the talk of individual children do give it the feel of being concerned with the individual, indeed with individual children. I have suggested that the authors do not quote in such a way as to substantiate that appearance. Moreover, the use they make of quotes is to demonstrate general theories. They do not give us three or four random pages of transcript of children talking and then see what can be said in a precise way about that talk using any one of several methods. They *start* with the theories, and the theorising constitutes the body of the text into which quotes are interpolated when 'suitable'. The form of the quotes is also made suitable. And there are suitable instructions in the body of the text to tell us how to read the quotes. The quotes are then a means to an end and appear in an end-structured argument. Methodologically they are redundant. They are not necessary. They are an encouragement to the reader-teacher to see further examples, they excite his experience, they talk of the individual but it turns out that their individuals do few of the things that individuals do. They resemble characters in allegorical tales — concepts in limited action rather than characters in complex interaction. And their speech is often used largely to support generalisations. Wayne Booth[39] talks in *The Rhetoric of Fiction* about 'telling' and 'showing' and of the ways that authors interfere with their characters. These authors interfere in a very gross way with theirs.

Now it may well be that the interference is justified. The dichotomic myth of research-here-presented vis-à-vis the real-research-which-is-too-long-complex-or-irrelevant-to-include-here encourages us to see that the authors have a whole bank of children's tapes which they have worked on in a methodical way; that their theories are the result of grappling with the data of such tapes; that these *transformations* of the data will actually give a more faithful rendition of the *character* of the data than *literal excerpts* from it; that to get a feeling of the *drift*, the *impetus*, the *essence*, the *import* of the research rather than the apparent facts, the surface phenomena, it has to be organised in such a way as these authors have done.

Rhetoric is a way to truth. Fiction too is a way to truth. Poetry, Surrealism, the picaresque, the allegorical are perhaps better ways to truth than the naturalist or realist novel. To say that this chapter of *Religious Education* is rhetorical, that it organises its characters like puppets to come in at various scenes of an argument and so on, need not be rude or diminishing. It is simply to re-categorise the chapter from being presented *research* to being *presented* research, and to draw a neglected attention to the methods of presentation. The chapter and its style of quoting are of particular interest in that they show the complex involvement of methods of recording data with data themselves, of both these with theorising, and of all three with presented argument. With the changes in the acceptability of different methodologies referred to earlier, extensive, linked quoting is a frequent characteristic of studies in education, insanity, community studies and deviance (in particular). Readers should interest themselves in the origin of that which is quoted, the form of the quote and the argumentative structure in which it is set.

## Sentimental Appeal

The use of child quotes has the rhetorical effect of bringing the reader nearer to the individual child and of showing the author closely linked with the child. It brings the subject matter alive and shows things which at least appear familiar. Here are real children with real names saying real things. What has not yet been explained and is much more difficult to explain is the sentimental effect of quoting. The quotes not only achieve verisimilitude in quickening the subject matter but they have the side effect of disposing the reader positively to the subjects, the children. We not only *feel* the reality, we *like* it. The quotes produce variations on the 'Ah, how sweet/clever/fascinating/funny' theme. This is partly explicable by the process described earlier in which the reader is invited to find order in the remarks and attribute that order to the child. Further, the chapter recalls work done by, for instance, anti-psychiatrists in its implicit contrast 'you may have thought children were just deficient adults but if you look closely enough you can see order in what they do'. The authors use the prose passages to help the reader see the achievements of the children and throughout the body of the text they stress positive things which children can do. Moreover, the graphical organisation of quoting in which the statement of the child is taken out of flow and set into the body of the text surrounded by white page encourages us to read the quote more slowly, more carefully than we might otherwise have done. Indeed, in some instances, this organisation, together with the internal organisation of the quote, transforms it into a sort of *epigram*. Thus the general 'pro-child' theme of the chapter, the instructions to find major things in the quotes (such as 'handling religious ideas') and the abstracted, isolated and emphasised presentation of the quote combine to dispose us towards its originator. This presentation highlights the slightly unusual use of familiar terms (see 'now and again' in the context of having babies) which we might otherwise miss. The epigrammatic form encourages us to read the quote as an insight rather than an odd, incoherent remark. And the quotes and the surrounding text show children doing nice things: they have ideas we adults can smile at ('I think God . . .'); they say sound, proverbial sorts of things ('Sometimes everybody makes a mistake'); they are humble ('I make mistakes'); they are alert to human suffering ('God makes mistakes like babies with no arms'); they 'show . . . continuing interest', they talk about 'mysteries' (curiously three children in a row talk spontaneously about mysteries); they are amusing ('why our mummy has babies now and again'); they are 'fascinated'; they 'question' and 'wonder'.

Clearly teachers and education researchers are going to be technically interested in the capacities of children. This chapter of *Religious Education* expressly sets out to describe the capacities of children at different stages of development. Equally clearly, some teachers and researchers will want to stress the positive capacities, the things children *can* do. But equally such an emphasis excites sympathies. It portrays children in such a way that the reader *feels* positively disposed to them. It directs sentiments. Wayne Booth again has noticed how our sympathies can be directed to bad characters whose badness is dramatised in certain ways:

> Macbeth's suffering conscience, *dramatised* at length, speaks a stronger message than is carried by his undramatised crimes . . . suppose he (the poet) wants his audience to pity what looks to any external view to be a vain man, or to love, as in Emma, what looks to any external view to be a vain and meddling woman – what then? Every resource of style, of transformed sequence, of manipulated inside views, and of *commentary* if need be – will be called in aid.[40]

The quotes help to dramatise the children. But these quotes also help to make them 'good'. Thus in two ways, in their achievement of 'reality' and positive sentiment they dispose the reader to the children and thus to the authors. Books with real characters are more interesting to read. Books with characters we can identify in our own lives and replicate are more 'relevant' to our 'needs'. Books in which the authors show a 'real' concern for their subjects excite our sympathies. Books in which our conventional sentiments towards the subjects are heightened leave us feeling good. All these things dispose us to the writer. For the interesting aspect of verisimilitude is that it reminds us that liking books is as important as believing them; and that liking them may help us to believe them.[41]

## Notes

1. These terms are borrowed from Dorothy Smith. D. Smith, 'K is mentally ill; the anatomy of a factual account', *Sociology*, vol. 12, no. 1, (1978).

2. See for one example A.V. Cicourel *et al*, *Language Use and School Performance*, (Academic Press, 1974). For an English example M.F.D. Young (ed.), *Knowledge and Control*, (Collier Macmillan, London, 1971).

3. Or claimed in such books as those in note 2 above to have been thought.

4. For an influential example, see the use made of perspectives in the Open University Course School and Society E282 original course.

5. As in Schools Council, Health Education Project 5-13, (Nelson, London, 1977).

6. As in Schools Council/Nuffield Foundation, *The Humanities Project: an Introduction*, (Heinemann, London, 1970).

7. As in Schools Council, *Religious Education in Primary Schools: Discovering an Approach*, (Macmillan, London, 1977). (My emphasis)

8. Schools Council, *Moral Education in the Secondary School*, (Longmans, London, 1972).

9. Schools Council, Research Studies, *Mass Media and the Secondary School*, (Macmillan, London, 1973).

10. See for example the way the Piagetian perspective is introduced in Schools Council, *Religious Education in Primary Schools: Discovering an Approach*, (Macmillan, London, 1977).

11. This is cogently argued by Sacks with regard to the problems of multiple descriptors in H. Sacks, 'Sociological Description', *Berkeley Journal of Sociology*, 8, (1963).

12. See Chapter Four. See also the analysis of chapter organisation in text books in D.C. Anderson, 'Literary and Rhetorical Features in the Local Production of a Sociological Argument', Doctoral thesis, (Brunel University, 1977).

13. See Chapter Two.

14. Garfinkel describes the characteristics of Et Cetera clauses in H. Garfinkel, *Studies in Ethnomethodology*, (Prentice Hall, Englewood-Cliffs, 1967).

15. See ibid. for an example.

16. As in the conversational analytic work of Sacks. H. Sacks, 'An Initial Investigation of the Usability of Conversational Data for Doing Sociology', in D. Sudnow (ed.), *Studies in Social Interaction*, (Free Press, 1972). See also J. Coulter, 'Harvey Sacks: a Preliminary Appreciation', *Sociology*, vol. 10 (1976), pp. 507-12.

17. D.C. Anderson, *Evaluation by Classroom Experience*, (Nafferton Books, Driffield, 1979).

18. M. Parlett and D. Hamilton, 'Evaluation as Illumination: a New Approach to the Study of Innovatory Programmes', Centre for Research in the Educational Sciences, University of Edinburgh, Occasional Paper 9, 1972.

19. At the time of writing, 1979.

20. For evidence of such feeling I rely mostly on teacher comments on panels during secondary school research 1977-80. Murdock and Phelps report similar comments in Appendix One of Schools Council Research Studies, *Mass Media*.

21. Schools Council, *Religious Education*, especially Chapter Three.

22. Ibid., p. 15, col. 1.

23. Ibid., p. 15, col. 2.

24. Ibid., p. 18, col. 2.

25. Ibid., p. 3, col. 1.

26. I use the term 'quasi-research' to relate to the notion of quasi-logical arguments referred to at the start of Chapter Two. The term is not abusive. Rather it draws attention to the fact that most actual published education arguments are neither totally 'impressionistic' (or whatever the opposite of logical is), nor are they either inductively or deductively logical. Their hybrid status is of interest because it raises the question of what are the criteria for assessing quasi-logical arguments?

27. See the section in Chapter Six p. 163.

28. Levi Strauss' work has been adapted for talk, particularly in the analysis of mass media, e.g. radio and television talk.

29. O. Holsti, *Content Analysis for the Social Sciences and Humanities*, (Addison Wesley, 1969).

30. R. Turner, *Ethnomethodology*, (Penguin, London, 1974) part IV.

31. D. Rummelhart, 'Notes on a Scheme for Stories', in D. Bobrow and A. Collins (eds), *Representations and Understanding in Cognitive Sciences*, (Academic Press, New York, 1975).

32. These stupefying effects can be seen in D.C. Anderson, 'The Classroom

as a Context for Health Education', in D.C. Anderson (ed.), *Health Education in Practice*, (Croom Helm, London, 1979).

33. Schools Council, *Religious Education*, p. 15, col. 2.

34. Ibid., p. 17, col. 2.

35. Ibid., p. 19, col. 1.

36. A point so simple and so important. I have to thank Wes Sharrock for emphasising it and its implications to me. I make it again in Chapter Six.

37. At the end of the excerpted section from p. 17.

38. This point is dealt with at length in Chapter Six. It also arises in D.C. Anderson, 'Curriculum Innovation and Local Need', *Journal of Curriculum Studies*, 11.2 (1979) and in D.C. Anderson, 'Curricula as Implicative Descriptions of Classrooms', No. 11, Occasional Papers, Leverhulme Health Education Project, University of Nottingham, UK (1978).

39. W. Booth, *The Rhetoric of Fiction*, (Chicago Press, Chicago, 1961).

40. Ibid., pp. 115-16, and quoted in D.C. Anderson, 'Borrowing Other People's Facts: The Case of Social Inquiry Reports', Paper given at the British Sociological Association, Annual Conference, (1979).

41. The general routine in this book is not to make use of privileged knowledge. However since the chapter in *Religious Education* not only uses children's quotes but is based on a borrowing from Piaget, and since my claim that borrowing 'cleans' materials by cutting out controversy needs some illustration, I refer here to well-known criticisms of Piaget summarised in two recent books. The books are too recent for the project to refer to but the criticisms are much older. M. Donaldson, *Children's Minds*, (Fontana Collins, Glasgow, 1978) especially Chapter 6, and M.A. Boden, *Piaget*, (Fontana Collins, Glasgow, 1979). Apart from these criticisms the last ten years have seen considerable work done on the problems of inferring capabilities, attitudes, etc. from talk. The authors ignore these.

The extract on pp. 132-3 is reproduced by permission from *Schools Council Religious Education in Primary Schools* (Macmillan Education, 1977).

# 6 THE RHETORIC OF PRACTICALITY

### Practicality

Curriculum projects may be based on excellent research and well argued but still faulted if they are 'impractical' or 'irrelevant'. In this chapter I wish to show what being practical is and just how difficult it is. In doing so I shall be implying that most curriculum books are not so much practical books as simplified 'theory'. They do, however, have a feel of practicality achieved by their doing things which are related to practicality but not sufficient for it. By showing just what practicality is and how far the books are from it, I suggest that this 'feel of practicality' is rhetorically contrived. Curriculum books wish to avoid the accusation of impracticality: further, being thought to be 'a practical book' may ease standards of 'academic' criticism as was suggested in Chapter Two.[1] There it was also argued that practicality is not equivalent to readability although it may involve it; that being liked by practitioners did not make a book practical although it might help it to be so; and that assurances that practitioners or observers had 'seen' a project being practised in the classroom should not be given automatic credence.

Practicality has to do with the book's suitability for its context of use. A practical book is one which can be used, which *fits* the actual circumstances of implementation. If it is a teaching book then the sort of model of a teacher its pages imply will be articulated to do the sort of things which actual teachers have to do; the model of a classroom its pages imply will be like actual or possible classrooms; the school organisation it implies will be like actual or possible school organisation; the community it implies is served by the school will be like actual communities and the dynamics of interaction between these and other items such as pupils will be like the dynamics of daily school life. This does not mean that the book will be like each particular school. But it does mean that the *forms* of daily life represented in the pages will resemble the forms of daily life within which real life decisions and actions are made.[2]

Daily school life *can* be pictured as a series of decisions or as a system of objectives but such pictures are inadequate and impractical. Formulating plans and intentions is one thing. Carrying them out is another. Daily life *is* concerned with planning, adopting perspectives and choosing strategies but it is more to do with adjusting plans to circumstances, with making the best of what one has got, with situated judgements about what is reasonable 'enough' in 'these' circumstances, about what can 'for now' be considered a reasonable substitute for X, about what 'doesn't matter too much', about 'what will do' and so on. Judgements in practical action are always based on what most theoreticians would see as inadequate evidence. They are made, so theoreticians would say, too hastily. Moreover most of them are made *during* the circumstances to which they apply. Decisions are made about pupils and topics *in* classrooms, at speed, based on a mixture of *practical* experience and the very immediate circumstances of *this* pupil's question, how much time is left and the noise coming from next door.

The practical world is often portrayed as a nuisance to the tidy world of theories. It is seen as deficient theory. Moreover, aspects of the practical world are seen as beyond or beneath theory. Theorists frequently point out that practitioners will have to fill in these missing parts themselves:

Consider the following: the first is from a D.E.S. Administrative Memorandum,[3] all the others from the School Council curriculum (in health education) for 9-13 year olds.

It is of course for local education authorities and schools to decide, in the light of local circumstances and the resources available, to what extent aspects of health education should be included in the school curriculum.

and

It is impossible and probably undesirable to offer a programme of health education which would be equally applicable to the many different schools and school organisations in the country. The shaping of such a programme can only be done by the staff of individual schools who are able to weigh the relevance and suitability of the materials, needs and background of the children involved. *It is for groups of teachers, therefore, to consider and use the guide in the light of their own situations.*[4] [Their emphasis.]

and

*Teachers are reminded, however, that the material is intended for guidance only and that they themselves must ultimately choose,*

*decide and plan what is appropriate for their children.*[5]
[Their emphasis.]

and

Any programme can only suit the particular school for which it
was designed — with its current staff complement, particular
needs, etc.[6]

One way to read these remarks is as those of a self-effacing
progressive central innovator humbly deferring to the
professionalism and local knowledge of the teacher 'in the field'.
The assumption is that at least some (unspecified) aspects of 'fields'
are different and that teachers are aware of them, and possibly, of
their 'difference'.

Another way to read the remarks is as the passing of a
monumental buck. The teacher is assigned a range of tasks awesome
in their methodological complexity, intransigent in their conceptual
confusion, a moral minefield to be negotiated without guidance but
within his free period. If we search the quotations and surrounding
texts for the methods by which teachers are to perform these local
adjustments we find no indication at all. Both D.E.S. and Schools
Council are simply agreed that adjustments are to be done 'in the
light'. Nor are they specific about the nature of the local situation to
be adjusted to. Their reticence is perhaps well advised for we shall
see that the question of adjustment is full of problems. To avoid
confusion let us clarify the nature of the innovators' omissions. It is
not, of course, that we expect them to know the particulars of each
locale. It is that they offer no notion of the methods by which
teachers may find, process and evaluate such particulars and then use
them to transform the initial curriculum.[7]

The article from which this excerpt is taken goes on to suggest the
extent of the job which innovators, or as I have been calling them,
theoreticians, are handing over to teachers. The innovator provides the
perspective and the materials and sometimes some in-service training.
The teacher has to take these and fit them into the cut-and-thrust of
daily life. This fitting operation will involve what some theoreticians
casually refer to as 'taking account of' circumstances. In the case of the
Schools Council Health Education Project (henceforth *Health
Education*) such circumstances include at the least, the mortality, and
morbidity figures and other contingencies of the catchment area

('community'), particulars of the school organisation, and of the classroom.

I shall argue in this chapter, with particular regard to practical activity in the classroom, that theoreticians have not begun to understand either the *amount* of work involved in this or the *type* of work involved in this. Following Garfinkel,[8] I shall insist that practical activity, the daily activity of teachers, is neither an untidy version of the plans, schemes and theories, nor is it beyond or beneath the capabilities of theoreticians. It is just that practical activity needs different theories and schemes to those commonly used.

Theories and schemes are often practical in that they address the topics of lessons or at least the titles of lessons. The curriculum projects talk about the topics which teachers use to describe their lessons (in some circumstances). The health education teacher can recognise that the Health Education Project 'contains' material on nutrition and he knows that he teaches nutrition. Moreover there may be a reciprocity of intentions or perspectives. The teacher may be able to see that the innovators want to obtain the same educational outcomes that he does. In both these senses and in the sense that he finds a project readable, its content familiar, and his fellow teachers consulted in it, he may find the project practical.

The missing element is form. It is not just that most innovators are not very concerned with the formal features of natural (i.e. non-experimental and non-abstracted) classrooms. It is that their irrelevance on this matter may destroy their relevance on the others. A practical curriculum proposal will have to take *form* seriously. It will have to start with the intransigent facts that daily life is not like theoretical life but that it *is* methodic. Despite its spontaneous, *ad-hoc*, contingent character, it is orderly, not chaotic. That orderliness comes from the fact that its participants synchronise their activities and judgements through concerted attention to the features of everyday life. They are 'experts' at it. A practical proposal will start with observations of how these experts do, in actual and natural settings, reasonably successfully 'muddle through'. A practical proposal will not be interested in the actual particulars which the practitioners have to deal with. But it will be interested in the *type* of particulars they have to be aware of. It will not list the varying attributes of different schools, communities and classroom but it will systematically examine the *type* of judgement that practitioners have to make about such things. In so doing it will not try to give them simplified models of theoretical decision-making to adjust, but itself investigate the business of making actual, daily, hurried, classroom decisions.

Projects do not typically start this way. They do not start with a prolonged and systematic observation and analysis of the reasoning that teachers employ about and in classrooms. They do not start with the contingencies of practical action, the contingencies which will define and limit other future action in these settings. They start with theories; theories about the subject matter, about the children, about the school, the community or learning. They start with reports: reports of what teachers, pupils or national agencies say they want, derived from questionnaires, interviews, official statistics and experiments. And their proposals are determined by their methods. In both theories and proposals the daily classroom world is cleaned of its reflexive, practical and interactional character. It is tidied into schemes, models, perspectives, lists, results, characteristics and correlations. It is proposed as a series of possible actions which take into account perhaps a learning model, perhaps the social background of the pupil, perhaps some other 'aspect' or 'factor'. But daily life is neither as simple as one factor nor do its practitioners get to choose which factor they consider. Daily life does not provide neat factors, its practitioners have to make instant and 'uninformed' decisions about which sort of behaviour 'this' action may reasonably, for practical purposes be considered an instance of.

It is not that life is complex and theories are neat. It is that the theories of the curriculum projects considered in this book show a minimal concern with the technicalities of daily life. Obviously, if they did address them, their job would be to simplify and 'code' them. There is nothing wrong with generalisation, simplification and coding. The objection is precisely that the theories have *not* systematically addressed the properties of daily classroom life. They are concerned with inputs and outputs, with possibilities, with conditionals, with models. They are concerned with 'the child', with 'learning', with anything other than the 'whatness', the 'quiddity'[9] of practical educational action in a given context. As a consequence they are relevant to teachers' *thinking* about children, classrooms and learning but, at least potentially, irrelevant to the *doings* of the classroom. And, as 'thinkings', they can only be translated into *doings* by a considerable effort during which they will radically and unpredictably change their character.

Practicality has to do with directness. The *original* writings of Plato, Piaget and Parsons are, in one sense of the word, relevant to the teacher in the classroom. In another sense we may talk of them being not directly relevant to the classroom teacher. In each of their cases, *work* has to be done to 'bring out' their contemporary and particular relevance. Steps have to be taken between the book and the classroom to associate the two more closely and precisely. In this sense they are not practical books. To say this is not in any way to abuse them. It is to note that books may be more or less *directly* and *explicitly* related to certain practical contexts. In the case of indirect, non-practical books, the question arises: 'Who will do this work of translating the book into the context?' And it is alleged to be one function of teacher-educators in universities and polytechnics to do just this. It is not too controversial to remark that not all students are always happy with the success of these relevancing operations and that may be a clue to just how big and difficult a task making things practical is.

Following the above definition, a non-practical book is one which requires substantial relevancing work to translate it into a form which fits the local context of use. It is further a book which leaves this work to someone else rather than doing it itself. In some cases the work is done orally by teacher-educators. In other cases we find books about books. For there are books which characterise themselves as bridging the gap between an original abstract book and a local practical context. They range from summaries to commentaries and from criticisms to outright manuals. The aim of such books is to be practical in the sense that the term is used above.

There is, however, another way of differentiating books, a way which is often confused with practicality and that is the criterion of simplicity. Blurbs of books often link the two together and in everyday talk one may often substitute for the other. We talk of 'simple, practical' guides. But, using the above definition, the two are not at all the same. A book may be a simple but very theoretical work and a manual may be very complex. Nor is practicality to be equated with a host of other criteria by which books are discriminated. These include, as discussed in Chapter Two, readability, familiarity and popularity.

The repeated conflation and confusion of these different criteria may explain why so many car-repair, cooking and camping, as well as teachers' manuals are bought with enthusiasm only to have their plastic ring spines broken in fits of despair at their subsequently encountered impracticality. They may display a picture of a car, a cooker, a tent or a pupil like ours on the front. They may be in simple English and they may have sold millions. But we cannot even turn their pages when the wind is howling round our collapsed tent and their ingredients are not available in our shops and there are always two sorts of the one they give and only one sort of the two they say are strictly necessary. It is a point worth serious attention that writing good practical manuals is very, very difficult. Academics tend to see manuals as the lowest form of literary life. But while there are many good academic education books available, the same cannot be said of manuals. Naturally if you know already and extensively how to repair your car or how to teach health education, a manual may come in most useful. Not only will it remind you about the size of bulb you need for X or the number of deaths from Y but, because you already know your subject and your task, you will be able to recognise familiar things in the manual and translate it yourself into practical action. Many manuals perform cataloguing and indexing tasks for existing experts very well. But their central task — helping someone who does not know it all to learn how to do it in his own natural circumstances — is less often well done.

One explanation for the failure of manuals is that the task they seek to do is enormously difficult. The practical world to which they try to adjust their methods and principles and perspectives is not only complex, but, particularly in the field of education, has not been thought worth studying. It has too many uncontrolled variables. It will not sit still. It does not have definite spatial temporal boundaries. It is topically 'confused'. With painstaking if unimaginative work one can simplify theoretical models for teachers. With a little style and a clear head one can make difficult writers readable. With a minimal imagination one can fill a manual with familiar examples. But helping with practice through a book is a different matter. That calls for an awareness of the working context of the practitioner and an ability to turn that intuitive awareness into an explicit description which captures the essence of what teaching is. That calls for a willingness to find methods which will handle this domain of the practical rather than changing one's domain of enquiry to suit one's existing methods. That calls, perhaps, for a reduction in the scope of one's innovatory horizons to fit the little one knows about practice. It is easy to see why the domain of the practical remains unpopular and unresearched. The cost of entering it is too great.

In Chapter Five the phenomenon of the borrowing of facts was discussed. It was implied that borrowing ought to be done according to some methodology because it was a complex operation which transformed the borrowed matters. Borrowing needs a methodology because it plays an important part in argument and because it is complicated. The translation of perspectives, concepts, intentions, theories, plans, policies, strategies and other agenda into the components of practical action is also a big and crucial process which needs a methodology. Most of the projects discussed in this book start with perspectives, concepts and such like and then claim to encapsulate these in teaching strategies and materials which in turn teachers are expected to adjust into practice. The translation exercise is thus thought of as shared between project members and teachers although it is rare to find the division of labour clearly and precisely spelled out. Whoever does the work of translating, it involves a range of obviously methodological operations such as:

1. Taking textual sketches of classrooms and their actors (pupils and teachers) and putting interactional flesh on them or, as I have expressed it earlier, articulating rather restricted primitive models of actors so that they can do the things such actors have to do in practice.
2. Developing a collection of procedures or rules in order to match intentions to actions and to substitute different actions as reasonable alternative strategies ('*different* ways of doing the *same* thing').
3. Developing practical measuring and assessing techniques so that, during action, one may decide that 'this' is 'enough', 'a lot', 'too much' or 'reasonable' and 'that' is 'good' or 'fair' or 'so bad that something must be done'.

If these sorts of tasks are involved in translating work and if projects claim to be doing a fair share of translating work then we will expect to find these tasks being done by projects. We will expect the curriculum projects to produce *lifelike* models of teachers, classrooms, and pupils. We will expect them to demonstrate explicit procedures and rules for strategy substitution. We will expect clear guides on the quantification, measurement and assessment of practical action. And if this sounds like a tall order it must never be forgotten that this is just the order that teachers have to meet in every class they teach. They have to make these decisions about what is to count as what, about what is interchangeable with what, about a lot, a little, about good and bad. Some of the talk about evaluation in teaching seems to ignore the fact that teachers are (intuitively perhaps) monitoring, judging, measuring, assessing, in fact reasoning about their work all the time. The work then *can* be done. The questions are: Do the projects play a part in this? If they do not, could they? And, more generally, is it reasonable to expect them or anyone else to write *explicitly* about practical reasoning? If it is, we can fairly expect curriculum projects with their self-styled practical emphasis, to be doing this work of explicating practice. If it is not, then we might ask what the projects *are* doing.

My view is that the curriculum projects do do some work in this area but not a lot. Moreover I think they choose the easier bits. Indeed, as the DES and Schools Council remarks quoted above reveal, so much is left to the teacher in the work of adjustment that it is highly dubious to say of any actual lesson that it is an instance of a particular perspective or project. The projects I consider are not and do not claim to be Platonic 'classics', discovering major truths about education. If they are not, in many ways, practical books, it is likely that in spite of their 'practical' form, their 'practical' claims and their 'practical' rhetoric, we should think of them rather as simplifications of 'theory' than as guides to practice. As such they have an enormous use but, except in certain areas where they do attend to practice (some indication of which is given below), that use is not directly practical. And to be fair, the interest curriculum innovators are now showing in in-service training can be seen as an admission of this. This interest can be represented as trying to do in another way what the *texts* largely failed to do — to get close to practice.

### Assessing the Practicality of Curriculum Texts

As Michael Eraut[10] has ably demonstrated, for the teacher, assessing whether a curriculum project is practical is largely a matching exercise in which the 'solutions' of the project are matched against the 'problems' of the teacher, classroom, school, pupil or community. With two minor modifications, the sort of approach he outlines can serve as an excellent guide on practicality assessment. First, not only the items of project and classroom but the character of each need to be compared and contrasted. Problems do not present themselves to the teacher singly as items but in groups. The problem is to do X while not doing Y but to do both before Z and in a hurry. But the teacher not only encounters several problems at once, the problems also combine in a *form* or a *constellation*. Anyone who assesses curriculum materials needs to be aware of these forms, these constellations and he needs to check to see whether the project has also seen fit to be interested in them.

Secondly, in order to match his 'problems' against the projects' preferred 'solutions', the teacher will need to draw up a list of each. Not only should his problem list contain forms of item combination as well as items, but the item should not be *surface* problems. I do not mean by this the usual rhetorical distinction of deep and surface problems nor the equally rhetorical presenting-as-opposed-to-real problem. At least, these are often rhetorical devices in which the arguer brands the problem he does not want to handle as surface or presenting and the one he prefers, or can find a solution to, as real or deep.[11] The distinction I draw is between 'problems' and the interactional and other factors which produce them. Insofar as problems occur in classrooms they emerge from constellations of dynamic factors, and insofar as solutions are to be attempted immediately or at least in the classroom it is to those factors that the practical project must address itself. (I do not concern myself with non-classroom solutions, which is a different matter).

The assessment of the practicality of curriculum projects will then itself involve a little study of the problem field and the solution text before matching the two. In the remainder of this chapter I suggest some directions for that study and illustrate some of the terms of this discussion such as 'producing factors', 'constellations' and 'easier bits'. The examples are taken from *Health Education*.

**Producing Factors**

Although teachers and curriculum innovators give titles to individual lessons and to courses, he would be a fool who thought that all the actions which go on during a lesson have to do with that title. Lessons include large numbers of activities and topics of talk which are not necessarily related to the subject-topic and lesson title or related to it in a sequential rather than a 'logical' way. My transcripts have handing back books, checking on absentees, exchanging greetings, talking about the time available and giving out resource cards, to name a few.

*Lessons are not Simply about their Titles and Topics*

Not only do lessons contain 'other' topics but they contain items which *produce* both the official and deviant topics. Lessons are started, utterances responded to, activities prefaced, topics initiated, speakers selected, items categorised in this way rather than that, pupil answers are assessed, 'corrected' and re-issued for the rest of the class, question sequences are set up, maintained and closed, monologues are constructed argumentatively and narratively and different actions are synchronised. This work on 'form' is not something separate from content. What we refer to as content is only recognisable through orientation to form. In this sense lessons are formal productions.

## Lessons Contain Formal Features which Produce Recognisable 'Content'

Although pupils and teachers may not be aware of it, they have to *work* in order formally to create the lesson. The work they do is collaborative. It is not that lessons have a teacher part and a pupil part. It is not even that these lesson parts are related. It is that collaboration is at utterance level. Teacher utterances speak cumulatively to last pupil utterances (and vice versa) to produce sensible orderly sequences of co-ordinated action. Of course, pupils do not always say or do what teachers want. But both speakers attend (or if they do not it is noteworthy) to what the other is doing — e.g. asking a question, replying, inviting, prefacing, exemplifying, listing — and they respond with a *sequentially relevant* if not *pedagogically desirable* action. This co-operative work, while it relies on general formal preferences, is particularly accomplished at utterance level. What will be a suitable rejoinder to other's utterance cannot be known until that utterance has been made. Thus the impression is both of orderly collaboration and of spontaneity. The lesson unfolds. Anything can happen. But whatever does happen, happens according to an orderly framework of preferences. A further impression is that, in keeping with the unfolding nature of the talk, the rightness or suitability of anything said is very much a located rightness. The problem is not so much what to say as when; or put as an issue for planners: how does one plan for the integration and maintenance of 'inputs' in an unfolding interaction where local relevance (that is local to the next utterance) is paramount? Consider as illustration of this theme, the profound effect of moving any of the utterances of the transcript (including later in this chapter) two, four or six positions forward or back. Moving them one, three or five positions would, of course, attribute them to a different speaker (pupils' to teacher's and vice versa) and that in turn raises the issue of how such speech actions as questioning, summarising, exemplifying, are tied to speakers' categories.

When I said that speakers collaborate with or address and attend to each other's talk utterance by utterance, I was not referring to hidden mental processes. The actions are observable by curriculum innovators. For speakers *display* their attention to each other in their rejoinders to them. This attention to last utterance is crucial. It is just not the case that teachers can say what they like. What they say is tied to, and can be seen to be tied to what has just been said. Even if teachers wish to ignore, disregard, deny, put down or destroy the last utterance, for example, a pupil's 'incorrect' or 'irrelevant' reply, they have to *do* ignoring, dismissing or whatever.

Classrooms are clearly unlike conversation then in that they have an agenda; in that utterance possibilities are strongly and discriminatively tied to speaker identities; in that next speaker selection is done by a specialised system. But they are like conversation and not, say, liturgical responses, in their unfolding unforeseeable character. Notice also that the collaborative and sequential nature of the talk makes suspect any unprincipled abstraction both of parts of and of complete utterances. Indeed, the presence of 'blocks' of questions, of chaining, and of common prefaces for more than two utterances, also makes suspect the abstraction of single pairs of utterances.

## The Production Work of Classrooms is Collaborative and Unfolding

Although teachers often say what the lesson will be about at the beginning, this announcement is not what makes the lesson 'about' its topic. This teacher's announcement of a lesson on understanding friends is immediately followed by an exchange about a pupil's whereabouts. This juxtaposition causes no distress whatsoever.

Tr. 1

| 1.9 | TV | . . . (find out where he is, in fact probably in a music lesson) Oh |
| 2.1 | P | Probably in a music lesson |
| 2.2 | TV | Oh is he now |
| 2.3 | P | He'll be here in about twenty minutes |
| 2.4 | P | ( ) |
| 2.5 | TV | Right, we're going to talk a bit about friendship <u>again</u>[12] |

Such phenomena indicate that preface, titles, etc. are not sufficient grounds for pupils to hear talk as about topic. The hearing of an utterance to be about X may be pre-signalled, but is also locally touched off. Similarly, local factors, in the extreme the utterance itself, are not, on their own, sufficient grounds for comprehension. Consider:

Tr. 2

| 2.5 | P | Proteins, fats, carbohydrates ( ) |
| 2.6 | A | Proteins, fats, carbohydrates |
| 2.7 | P | Vitamins |

| 2.8 | A | Vitamins |
|-----|---|----------|
| 2.9 | P | Mineral salts |

or again in Tr. 1 we find:

| 7.3 | TV | Anyone want to say anything about threes being in friends of threes . . . |
|------|----|------|
| ([Four utterances]) | | |
| 7.8 | P | Yeh since I started to make friends and broke friends and made it then broke then made it again |
| 7.9 | TV | Em |
| 7.10 | P | You see and when I wasn't his friend he'd played football you see and he started to make up then |
| 7.11 | TV | Em |
| 7.12 | P | And then gave me a bit of (company) and then so so |
| 7.13 | TV | Em |
| 7.14 | P | It didn't eh come out in a fight |

Teachers and pupils manage to 'understand' each other's remarks, at least insofar as to be able to produce a sequentially suitable rejoinder, although those 'understood' remarks are frequently neither in a conventional syntactic form nor lexically clear. In Tr. 2 above, the items in 2.5, 2.7 and 2.9 are part of a list made collaboratively with the teacher (A), a list grammatically incomprehensible but understood by at least some of the participants, through attention to preface, to the identity of the speakers. This quality of utterances highlighted in TV's instructions to continue talking 'Em' and the teacher repetitions in Tr. 2, is referred to as indexicality. Participants' 'problems' with such utterances are not only or necessarily with their meaning but with what to do next. They could sit and stare at the individual utterances and they would never know. They can inspect the preface and that will be insufficient. Only by attending to both preface, utterance and the intermediate stretch in their formal sequential and categorical development will participants find what they have to do next.

Another aspect of the indexical character of utterances is that two different lexical or grammatical units can do the same work. Consider at least some similarity in the work (as continuation markers) done by 'Em' and the repeats in Tr. 2 to instruct current speaker to continue. Likewise, similar lexical items and syntactic structures can do different work if spoken by a different speaker if in a different 'chain' of utterances, if preceded by a different preface, if followed by a different retroactive 'correction' (such as a tag) and so on. For example, P's 'Proteins, fats, carbohydrates' is an answer and addition to a list, also a type or category setter for guidance as to the production of suitable next items on the list, while A's production of exactly the same words in the same order and structure is a several-duty utterance doing acceptance of offered answer, instructions to last or another speaker to offer more of the same, etc. I am not relativising the lesson so as to say, e.g. 'anything can be anything and mean anything'. Clearly it cannot. Manifestly, the organisation of talk in these lessons is orderly. What I am claiming is that this orderliness is not produced by 'keeping to a lesson plan' or simply using teacher authority to announce what will happen or what will be said, or to direct the course of the lesson. Nor is it achieved by virtue of the manifest functions of lexical items and syntactic structures. If the lesson proceeds and unfolds as an orderly phenomenon, it does so not by virtue of what has obviously 'been said' or the obvious 'role of the teacher', not by mechanisms we can dismiss or take for granted, but by the stepwise attention of participants to the formal structures of the interaction. To 'introduce' a syllabus or agenda into the classroom is to introduce it into such orderly interaction. We may choose whether to do this blindly or in some knowledge of the structures of that interaction. At the present most curricula do not even refer to it even to dismiss it.

## Lessons Unfold in an Orderly Way

Several teachers and co-researchers commented that the transcripted lessons were 'busy', that a lot happened. One way of evidencing this might be to count utterances and show that, for example, Tr. 1 (in its entirety) has 295 in about 30 minutes, or one every six seconds. But as we have noted repeatedly, lessons are not made up of individual, but of linked, often paired utterances, in Sacks's term 'adjacency pairs'.[13] They consist of interaction, not unbroken monologue. The different parties to this talk may say what they want to say (who can tell?) but they *form* their utterances in the light of preceding interaction, especially the immediately preceding utterances. The 'busyness' of Tr. 1 is then, as much as the 295 utterances, the 294 sensitive and orderly *transitions*. At each transition 'solutions' are found to the 'problems': when is this utterance finished and when can I start speaking? Who is to speak at the transition relevance place? What was the last utterance doing and what am I required to offer as a paired next utterance? As one may see from the transcripts, utterances in these particular lessons follow swiftly on the heels of preceding utterances, nor is there such confusion as would be evidenced by overlapping talk to any degree. These problems are routinely solved. They are not solved by silence distribution, although silences do occur, and they are solved quickly. The speedy resolution of these problems, particularly the third, is of special note when made by the teacher. If it is wished that teachers' assessments of pupil utterances should be guided by project perspectives and educational aims, it should be explained how this can be done immediately, for immediacy is the most notable character of assessment as practised.

## Lessons are Busy

Insofar as the teacher makes instant assessments of pupil utterances evidenced by the speed of speaker transitions and the paired character of utterances, teacher utterances are not *any* utterances, but utterances which speak immediately to the preceding. In the case of utterances with no gap, it is tempting to infer that either teachers project the last section of pupil utterances and formulate their own during the course of the pupil utterance, or that they start their own utterances not knowing how they are to finish. It is this character of teacher talk and assessment which is so unlike the scenic implications and assumptions of both curriculum designers and teacher-trainers. It may be important to use pupil utterance to find its speaker's 'ability' on topic. It may be important to assess the effect of accepting/rejecting that answer on the producer's future forthcomingness and involvement. It may be important to assess the effect of such a teacher endorsement on the rest of the pupils, or its implications for the coherence of topic to date and agenda to come. What is apparently crucial is that each and all of these be done immediately — NOW. One can offer then to curriculum innovators a new and awesome vision of 'continuous assessment'. Such assessments, like the other features we have seen, display the class as at once an unfolding accomplishment and a formal structure and the teacher as *systematically ad hocing* his way through the lesson. Lessons then are not idiosyncratic but systematic: the system is not the one in the rationalist planner's manual and diagram:[14, 15] nor is it the system implicit in the project's models.

## The Teacher's Business is Instant Reply and Instant Judgement

Up to this point I have concentrated on showing that lessons display an extensive, sensitive and systematic regulation that is not spoken to in curricular texts. The implicit analogy has been of cog wheels already turning (the interactional system) into which any new item (topic, title, agenda, syllabus) must be fitted or tailored or turned so as not to be crushed, but to enmesh. Without being over-refined, we might note some problems with this analogy. First, the agenda is presumably part of the system, not something introduced to it. Secondly, insofar as the system can be conceptually discriminated from the agenda, we have not two items, but at least three:

1. Topics, agendas, etc.
2. Interactional systematics common to talk on many unscripted occasions.
3. Patterns of interaction more particular to lessons or parts of lessons.

The lesson is then talk, lesson-talk and topical-lesson-talk. Even this is an unsatisfactory way of describing it since it presents these aspects as simply conjoined, whereas topic talk is done *through* general and particular systematics of talk. Topic talk is done by talking topically.[16]

## Topic and Form are Enmeshed[17]

These glimpses of actual lessons reveal characteristics which do not seem to be addressed by project models to any extent. Project models of lessons tend to talk about either the subject-topic or about cognitive and 'educational' activities, whereas what the teacher has to deal with are not only contingent constellations of interactions but the relationships between these, his own intentions and 'educational' interpretations. Secondly, projects tend (even the 'liberal' ones) to give the teacher an unrealistic type of power. It is not that teachers have or should have more or less power than the projects suggest. It is that the type of power they have to 'do things' is much more hedged about by interactional particulars than the projects suggest. The collaborative, unfolding nature of classrooms need not limit the teacher's power to introduce a new topic or perspective but it modifies the exercise of that power in a complex of ways. Thirdly, the instantaneity of lessons is something that projects do not seem to address. They are concerned with the 'right' 'educational' way to do things. Teachers are concerned with the apt, immediate way to do things. And fourthly, and lastly, the projects imply a planning process which does not fit actual lessons. In actual lessons the difficult task is not formulating a plan, sub-strategies, educational techniques and aids, it is the maintenance and continuous adjustment of plans, intentions and agenda during the interaction of the lesson. In summary, the models of projects and the reality of lessons diverge sharply at least over the practical area of classroom interaction. And in this field it is the teacher who does most of the translating work. This does not mean that the projects offer nothing.

## Projects and Teachers

### Health Education as decision making

There is a growing tendency today to place the major responsibility for individual and communal health upon the health services and the personnel who man them. There is a consequential reluctance to accept that our 'health' is largely dependent upon the choices and decisions we ourselves make from day to day. Essentially health education should be seen as providing planned experiences for children on matters concerning their present and future health. Its major aim should be to help children make considered choices or decisions related to their health behaviour by increasing knowledge and clarifying the beliefs and values which they hold. Health education, in our view, should not only concern itself with the passing of information but should also involve children in the process of making choices or decisions.

Children need to be called upon to use what they know, and to make choices in a considered and productive way so as to involve them personally, both individually and in groups. The strategies to be found in each of the eight units have been designed to emphasize the personal involvement and responsibility of children and call for investigation, judgement, choices and decisions of various kinds. All the units contain material to be 'learned', but, equally important, they offer opportunities for children to put what they have learned to some use in a way which is relevant and meaningful to them. Such an interpretation of school health education reflects the growing awareness amongst teachers of the need to develop in children a sense of personal involvement and responsibility for their own health.[18]

This section is easily *readable* and it is *simple*. If we know that there is a considerable literature on decision-making and values-clarification in health education and that these are names of schools of thought rather than terms invented by the author, we can see the authors introducing the reader to some major issues of health education in a simple and unpretentious way. The terms are titular, coming as they do in the introduction. We are going to hear more about them. Since the piece is a sort of preface, it cannot fairly be expected to contain examples and instances. Nor can we expect it to be sensitive to the complexities of classroom context. Yet even in such a preface an issue of practicality does arise.

The piece is very ideological. It represents one popular view about the functions of school education. While not narrowly so, it is child-centred, pro pupil 'activity' pro the 'involvement of the child's non-school experience' and so on. Not only does it explicitly adopt this ideology. It also contains lots of words associated with such an ideology such as 'relevant', 'groups', 'experiences', 'meaningful' and 'involvement'. These words are recognisable as, at least, *not* the vocabulary of some other positions. In setting up these principles of good education, the project implicitly offers to reader-teachers a useful methodological tool with which to scrutinise their activities. They can ask of their class: 'Did it provide for pupil choices?' 'Did it speak to the child's outside experience?' 'Was it relevant?' etc.

While the actual structure of *Health Education* is complicated (it uses two of its units to mediate between the introduction and the strategies), the whole project does go some way not only to giving teachers such general questions to ask, but, at least implicitly, to suggesting ways they might be able to answer them. The project does not only give abstract principles. It gives them as possible methodological tools and it helps the teacher apply these to his work, so that the teacher may say of the project that it gave him new intentions, new materials and new ways of seeing whether his efforts have incorporated his intentions (although the last is largely intuitive and implicit). In these areas the project is practical and useful.

In two ways though, the project is not practical. First, and of lesser importance, the contrast set up in the introduction piece between passing information and decision-making, while theoretically fascinating, is extremely difficult to apply to actual lessons. It is a contrast that comes from 'theory': it is not the most obvious way one would divide health education lessons up if one looked at the lessons themselves. Looking at tapes of health education lessons there are lots of ways one might allocate them into contrastive classes but this is not one of them. It is, of course, a distinction that health educators are obsessed with and a distinction which derives from *experimental* settings in which either tests or classrooms are contrasted under the two headings. The conventional wisdom is that 'just' passing information is not enough, even changing attitudes may not be enough: health educators should be concerned (if they are 'authoritarian') with modifying behavioural outcomes, or (if they are 'liberal') with helping people to make more mature or productive decisions. The problem is to find a classroom in which the lesson is 'just passing information' and to locate *directly* an instance of decision-making. Both information retention and decision-making are essentially post hoc analytic processes constructed on the basis of contrasts between two items of talk or text. Ironically, both use the same 'data' as a base from which to infer themselves. They are not so much contrasting activities as metaphorical ways of interpreting classroom talk. While they can be closely defined into experimental contrast, they are very difficult to operate within a natural classroom. They are none the less beguiling and it is possible for the enthusiastic teacher to 'see' decision-making as the work of his classroom without any similar observation being made by other observers.

The distinction between the two is also part of a wider distinction between active and non-active classrooms, referred to by the authors under the term 'involvement'. Pupils are not supposed to sit and passively 'receive' information but to involve themselves actively in the learning process. This is also difficult to apply in practice largely because passive learning is a contradiction in terms (at least in classroom rather than KGB conditions) and thus the notion of active involvement is redundant and trivial. Of course, it is possible for pupils not to be involved in the *way* that teachers would wish but that is a different matter. The distinction is difficult to apply because:

1. There are many ways for pupils to be 'involved', most of which are not monitorable, at least during lessons, by teachers.
2. Classrooms are full of activities even if not the official ones.
3. All understood, i.e. learned talk is implicative of action and decision. It involves the reader in adjusting it 'for himself' into his scheme of relevances; his monitoring it to see what is required of him next and so on. Moreover the retention and re-issue of 'information' require active processes. Even the activities of disattending then re-attending at crucial moments are active involvements in the lesson.

Projects may make distinctions between more-preferred and less-preferred activities. They cannot reasonably and relevantly make distinctions between active, involved pupils and non-active, non-involved pupils. Teachers' problems derive from actions which they cannot monitor or do not like, not from inaction. None of this prevents us from using inaction as a euphemism for unmonitored, unmonitorable or unapproved action. Nor does it stop us 'seeing' a particular classroom as an instance of the 'decision-making approach'. But both euphemism and vision will be trivial for they will confuse ways in which classrooms *can* be described with the factors which actually produce classroom activities. They will be like those elegant theorists of language who, having produced complex theories of the structure of language, go on, ludicrously, to suppose that children actually learn language by such structures.[19]

The contrast in the *Health Education* piece does not, I think, originate in classroom observation and it cannot be applied to classrooms *as it stands*. It is, like the rest of the piece, not really about classrooms at all. If we ask what the piece is about, we will reply that it is about teachers' intentions. It is suggesting that teachers adopt certain intentions — intentions to promote certain 'cognitive' changes, actions and choices in their pupils. It is a proposal about intentions and plans. As such it speaks to that part of the teacher's role which is concerned with planning, making 'policy', adopting approaches and intending. Crudely, it is about *things teachers do before they enter the classroom*. Insofar as it addresses the actual business of the classroom, insofar as it addresses the *doing* of the project rather than the thinking about prior to, or the telling about after the lesson, it is largely concerned with setting up tasks.

## Another Contrast: the Work of the Project and the Work of the Teacher

Consider this extract from a curricular project:

> The pictures on Resource Sheets 42 and 43, shown on pages 7 and 8, are offered for use as triggers for the children's own investigations. Each picture is accompanied by comments or questions relevant to the question "Why do we eat?". It is suggested that this material should provide activities for groups or individual research, but it is not intended that *all* children should attempt *all* the activities. A display of group or individual work or a discussion arising out of the work should serve to focus the children's attention on the major issues of why we eat food.
>
> Teachers might also encourage children to collect their own pictures of food being eaten in differing circumstances.
>
> Ask the children to group the pictures in response to the

question: why do we eat food? Two categories might be suitable.
1. To keep alive.
2. For enjoyment.

## Picture 1

This provides for discussion of the instinctive drive to search for food. Babies are born with a sucking reflex — that is, they suck at things put into or near to their mouths. Indeed, babies also 'search' for their mothers' breasts.

Teachers might encourage children to find out how the instinctive drive for food finds expression in some other animals — chicks with beaks wide open when hungry, newly-born puppies searching for their mother's nipples, etc. One interesting instinctive drive is that shown by the herring gull chick which pecks at any red spot it sees. The mother's beak has a red spot which when pecked by the chick stimulates the mother to regurgitate food. The regurgitated food is then eaten by the chick.

The children might also be encouraged to collect pictures of newly born or very young animals feeding.

## Picture 2

Babies cry when they feel hungry but gradually adjust to the routine of proper meal times. Children often develop a 'sweet tooth' because parents give them something sweet (chocolate, sweets or a dummy dipped in honey) when they claim to be hungry between meals.

## Picture 3

There are many opportunities for buying snack foods, ice cream and sweets, etc. Children do not usually see items such as hamburgers, chips and hot dogs as real meals, although they are often fairly substantial.

## Picture 4

Following the theme of eating to keep alive, it is of interest to discuss how man is able to survive in the most difficult situations by using technology — in this instance food technology. Other activities which are assisted by the development of food technology are mountaineering, pot-holing, sailing, caravanning, etc.[20]

Illustration

## Why do we eat?:1     `RESOURCE SHEET 42 UNIT 6`

**1**

What is this baby doing?

How often is a young baby fed?

Can you think of how some baby animals feed?

**2**

At what age can children feed themselves?

Do they eat the same kinds of food as adults?

What food do they eat and why?

What happens if they feel hungry between proper meal times?

**3**

What foods are sold from stalls, kiosks and mobile vans?

Which of these is your own favourite, and which are the most popular in your class?

When are these foods most usually eaten?

How much of their pocket money do many children spend on foods like these?

**4**

Why aren't astronauts able to eat ordinary foods?

What kinds of food are they able to have?

What kinds of food take up the least space and are light in weight?

What other activities are helped by food which is specially prepared?

The actual strategies of the project help the teacher set up tasks or activities. The project suggests an activity and then proceeds quite logically to tell the teacher how it may be started. The teacher already has received useful help from the project on perspectives and intentions. Now it gives him some materials and suggests some initiatives. Actual classroom life does not start, at least in this 'clean' way. It is part of continuing activities. The participants and the interaction have biographies and histories and the first translating work of the teacher will be in amending the starts-from-scratch of the project to starts-from-where-we-are. This work is not really starting at all but turning a start into a development. And even with starts it becomes quickly obvious that the problem is not initiation of the activity but maintenance and development. Here is a teacher introducing a lesson which uses cards from the Health Education Project:

Tr. 1.

1.9　TV　Did you hear what she just said — there is a point which
　　　　　I haven't told you about yet, I haven't shown you it
　　　　　(　　　　　　　　　) that perhaps it might have been a
　　　　　bit of a lie if I let it go on (　　　　　　　　). Anyway,
　　　　　while we wait for em David and Paul to come up I
　　　　　thought rather than just a general discussion <u>again</u> I'd
　　　　　give you something to get it to go = ( [volume increase] )
　　　　　it's a bit of a similar subject to before and it's called
　　　　　'understanding friends' = now we've talked a little bit
　　　　　about friends before so em if this would be OK with
　　　　　you eh Dr. *** we'll I'm going to give everybody a card
　　　　　and rather than perhaps dividing you into little groups
　　　　　we'll try and discuss it in a big group first of all and then
　　　　　if you would like to go off into small groups eh discuss
　　　　　it on your own afterwards so let me just hand out these.
　　　　　Have a look — partly, have a think and then we'll go
　　　　　round and get a discussion going. There are girls things
　　　　　and boys things so let's give the girls . . . (find out where
　　　　　he is, in fact, probably in a music lesson). Oh . . .

TV is a school counsellor with a small class of twelve-year-olds. The
lesson lasts about 25 minutes and consists of 280 utterances.
Although that produces a mean utterance time of some 5.4 seconds,
teachers' utterances are typically slightly longer than pupils'.
Twenty-eight of her 140 are longer than 25 words while only eight
of their 140 utterances are longer than 25 words. What this amounts
to is that the bulk of the lesson is kept going by short elliptical
remarks:

Tr. 1 20.3 to 20.17

20.3　TV　Can anyone else give some examples of gossip that
　　　　　doesn't matter — wouldn't upset someone. What about
　　　　　yourself what wouldn't you mind people saying about
　　　　　you — behind your back?
20.4　P　　Hmmm.
20.5　TV　It's rather difficult to answer that question isn't it.
20.6　P　　(Because it's liable)
20.7　TV　Is there anything that = do you think we shouldn't talk
　　　　　about any of us I mean we could just send one person

out one out of (the class) one after the other and have a
gossip about them while they weren't here.

| 20.8 | P | It's good that |
| 20.9 | P | ([Laughter]) |
| 20.10 | TV | Paul says it's all right |
| 20.11 | P | (You go out) |
| 20.12 | P | (You go after us then) |
| 20.13 | P | No |
| 20.14 | P | Yeh go on |
| 20.15 | P | Ha ha |
| 20.16 | P | After you |
| 20.17 | P | Who's next? |

And not only are there lots of short utterances but they usually
follow hard on each other's heels. The total time for the ten
utterances 20.8 to 20.17 is about five seconds. Thus when we follow
the lesson through saying such things as 'the teacher opens the
lesson, gives out some situation cards, asks a series of questions
about each card then closes the lesson' we have a vision of the lesson
consisting of several parts such as: introduction, distribution,
discussion and collection of cards; and closure. But within these
'parts' there may be some 60 utterance transitions and that means
sixty occasions on which the teacher has to decide what to say,
whether and how to prompt, to accept or reject 'answers', what to
say that might 'help' the next pupil see the personal relevance of the
situation under discussion, etc.; or, seen another way, sixty
occasions on which the lesson could change direction and become
something different. These figures are not, of course, given for
themselves, but as an image of the sort of process that is going on in
this lesson. What we are saying is that division of lessons into parts
or objectives is certainly useful in order to talk about them (or
something!) afterwards but that it comes nowhere near capturing
the interactional zig-zag of a lesson. All of which is but a preface on
how to read this account of a lesson which inevitably talks about it
as if it were a series of parts.

TV opens with some business about the tape-recorder (utterances
1 to 8) then does an introductory monologue which has to do with
checking who is there, mentioning the subject to be discussed and
tying it to a subject they have talked about before 'understanding
friends'. During this business it turns out that one pupil is missing
and the first topic discussed in the lesson is his whereabouts.

The 'main' topic is then reintroduced and instructed to
start:

Tr. 1 2.5

2.5   TV   Right it's very similar let's just eh can you look up
a minute — it's fairly similar it's again about friends em
but you might have got quite a lot of ideas about this
one. What I'll do is ask one person in turn just to
describe it to the rest of us and then we'll get going.
Carolyn would you like to just wave the picture at us so
that we can see what it's about — and just read the
(                              ) underneath.

Carolyn reads the caption:

Tr. 1 3.1

3.1   P   Barbara's my best friend and we have known each other
since infant school. I know that she wants to be friends
with a new girl here who is very popular with everybody
but I had arranged to go out with Barbara on Saturday
night but at the last moment she said that she couldn't
because her grand-parents were visiting. Then I saw her
in the town with Liz shopping.

The teacher 'paraphrases' the caption for the pupils. Throughout our
tapes these paraphrases are frequent. Teachers not only paraphrase
materials for pupils but other pupils' remarks. In so doing they draw
attention to some features of the remarks and materials and play
down others. It is tempting to theorise about the work such
paraphrasing does. Certainly it is frequently used to personalise the
materials, to turn them into 'our' matter rather than someone else's
by, for example, replacing fictional names with pupil names. It may
simplify materials perhaps by suggesting a sequential order in which
they should be taken. And in the case of paraphrases of pupil talk,
teachers may use the paraphrase to endorse what has been said, to
increase its audibility and so on. Paraphrases occur because of the
particular nature of (most) classroom turn-taking in talk whereby
teacher frequently speaks each alternate turn. For us, their
immediate interest is in their demonstration that lesson themes and
topics are not introduced into classrooms simply through curriculum
materials or introductory talk but that what-a-lesson-is-about and
what-we-are-doing-now are matters produced by teachers throughout

the lesson. Put more simply, if lessons appear to flow and to stay
on topic, then that appearance is the result of teacher efforts
throughout the lesson and not simply of curriculum planning.

After the paraphrase, Carolyn is asked to read the first question:

Tr. 1 3.5

3.5   P     How did the girl feel about her best friend Barbara called
            Barbara when she saw her out with Liz?

Once again the teacher paraphrases:

Tr. 1 3.6

3.6   TV    So how would you feel if you sudd . . . if you'd asked
            your best friend to do something, they said they
            couldn't and then went out with someone else? ( [0.10] )
            Has this ever happened to you?

and gets

Tr. 1 3.7

3.7   P     No.

She tries again:

Tr. 1 3.8

3.8   TV    Well try and imagine it then. Have you got any special
            friends? Who is one of your special friends?

and again:

Tr. 1 3.10 after no discernible response.

3.10  TV    Suppose you ask Tracy to do something with you and
            she said sorry she couldn't and then you saw her out
            with someone else how would you feel?

After an incomprehensible response, she tries yet again:

Tr. 1 4.1 to 4.2

4.1   P     (                              ) why she lied to me
4.2   TV    Would you — would you feel upset or angry?

This is greeted with silence and after ten seconds she makes another
attempt:

Tr. 1 4.3

4.3   TV    Is there anyone in the room who has had that sort of
            thing happen to them perhaps when they were in

junior school? ([0.10]) What's happened to you
(                              ).
How did you feel when that happened to you?

After some 40 utterances into the lesson she starts to receive
utterances on which she can build and re-offer further questions so
that gradually the materials are left behind. The responses become
longer and more developed and faster. Pronoun usage and topic
change so that it becomes clear that the pupils are talking about
themselves (their homes, parents, etc.) rather than the pictures on
the cards. This 'achievement', the result of considerable hard work,
is not without its problems. Some pupils have news about
themselves which they feel is crucial but which bores everyone else.
Some have interesting news but are incompetent story-tellers. Others
tell interesting and captivating stories but the moral is impossible to
make out. Once again the teacher continuously monitors: reworking
this pupil utterance, noticeably not reworking that, pulling out
morals-for-us-here-now but keeping her responses such as not to
discourage both individuals and the general flow of talk. The
sophistication of the teacher's intervention resides not only in what
she says and noticeably does not say but in when she talks and
when she noticeably does not talk:

Tr. 1 8.3 to 9.2

| 8.3 | TV | No. What do you think grown-ups do when they fall out? Do you think teachers, men teachers sort it out with a scrap or . . .?<br>([Laughter]) |
|------|------|------|
| 8.4 | P | Might do |
| 8.5 | P | They ignore each other. |
| 8.6 | TV | They'd ignore each other. Yes — till they'd both cooled down do you mean. |
| 8.7 | P | Yes |
| 8.8 | P.1 | That's what my sister does — she ignores me. |
| 8.9 | | ([Laughter]) |
| 8.10 | P.1 | She put . . . she threw a table at me once.<br>([Laughter]) |
| 8.11 | TV | How cruel. |
| 8.12 | P | Could have killed me. |
| 8.13 | TV | Did you do nothing to make her angry. |
| 8.14 | P | (Course he did [Laughter]) |

8.15   P.1   Well, I like, I like bullying her.
8.16   TV    Ah I see.
9.1    P     She's twice as old as him.
             ([Laughter])
9.2    TV    Maxine

At the same time as monitoring the timing of talk and the topic, the teacher is doing a sequential and predictive analysis, looking to see how what is being said fits with what has been said, looking to the time left in the lesson, to what will happen if she lets X continue to talk, to her own next response. She also has to allocate turns to talk among the pupils, sometimes in the face of competition. Frequently she accompanies such allocations with justifications:

Tr. 1 17.12

17.12 TV   I'd better have Diane because she had her hand up.
           Diane then Aden. ([laugh])
           (                        ) you've had your hand up so long.

Such allocations can, as any of the business of the lesson can, at any time, become a matter themselves for discussion:

Tr. 1 17.13 to 18.2

17.13 P     Let Aden go
17.14 TV    OK Aden first then Diane
17.15 P     (I forgot what I was going to say)
            ([Laughter])
18.1  TV    Oh Diane's remembered.
            ([Laughter])
18.2  P     Em my friend is always talking about me (Chris told me)
and such business talk needs to lead back to topic talk as here.

And so it goes on until the teacher's monitoring of talk so far, time ahead and talk to come, together with her assessment of current talk, suggests that she close the section and have the pupils look at another card.[21]

TV's lesson was a lesson which made good use of resource cards (both in the piece transcribed here and even more so in the remainder of the lesson). But the point of interest in it for this argument is the sheer amount of work that TV has to do, work which is not provided for in project books. For her, a lot of the work was 'routine' and a lot, if not intuitive, was certainly done without 'noticing'. Her start took time, effort and skill. And as the lesson went on there were more and more complicating factors to which, and to the constellations of which, she had to respond. Her main task and the task which influences *all* her other tasks was the maintenance and development of the lesson. Projects are curiously silent on this area. They talk of perspectives, of plans and of starts, of activities, but then are silent until the next activity starts. These next activities also start 'out of the blue' and are maintained and finished by teachers unaided by project advice.

It will of course be argued that lesson maintenance is not the job of curriculum projects; that it is work for teacher trainers. But I will maintain that to set aside lesson maintenance is not only to leave the majority of the translating work to the teacher but to undermine the overall practicality of the project, leaving it as a useful simplification of theory, an enticing perspective to help teachers think and intend, a set of materials for them to use but not a practical project. In short, the two things projects wish not to be, simplified theories or tips for the teachers, they court by their lack of practical advice on the maintenance of perspectives, plans and intentions during lessons.

It has also to be said that a project which did address maintenance might be thought to encroach on teacher autonomy. Those offering practical advice run the paradoxical risks of being rejected by practitioners for being distant and irrelevant or for being too close for comfort. Practicality tends to be one of those things people ask for, secure and relieved in the knowledge that it will not be delivered.

## Postscript

Is the criticism that curriculum texts tend to a merely rhetorical practicality a pejorative one? Indeed are any of the characteristics attributed to curriculum texts — quasi-science, artful borrowing, verisimilitude, persuasion through textual layout, graphics, sequential organisation, selective categorisation through creative representation of the research base and so on — are these characteristics to be seen as faults? Obviously in one sense they cannot be faults. Many of them are simply the inevitable result of writing books in ordinary language. One cannot clean ordinary language or the reading practices of ordinary readers of such characteristics. Generally it is not a fault that curriculum texts are rhetorical and certainly the five texts studied are not at fault. Yet, while it is the least important aspect of rhetoric in curriculum texts, the question is bound to be asked whether the rhetorical character of the texts has any implications for judgement of such texts. And I do think that in two senses the criticisms of curriculum proposals made in this book do not simply 'illuminate' the kind of product that curriculum books are: they have something damaging at least to imply about them and their discipline. First, if the persuasive basis of the texts is at least partly rhetorical and only partly 'scientific', the claim of the texts to be based on 'research' must be only partly upheld. Moreover, since the texts' proponents do not show how the rhetorical and scientific parts relate, the research is not only *partly* based on 'research' but *confusedly* based on it. Thus an awareness of the part played by rhetoric might suggest that curriculum proposers be more modest about their products.[22] Their 'research' has 'shown' little and proved less. It is not a firm basis for their proposals. Such proposals should be more in the nature of pursued hunches, thoughtful suggestions and helpful hints. As such, their scope should be more limited, their field of application narrower and more gradual.

Secondly, if curriculum arguments and indeed most education arguments are both currently rhetorical and likely to remain so, then the discipline, if it wishes to develop sound criteria for its arguments, must *work* to develop them. That task will involve studying how its arguments do work before deciding which practices are good and bad and permissible or not. The relevant question is not whether *I* intend these rhetorical analyses of curricular text pejoratively, but whether the discipline is prepared to treat its inevitable rhetorical component seriously and incorporate it in its critical standards. So far it has not, in general, done so and that is clearly and extremely unsatisfactory.

## Notes

1. Chapter Two, p. 55.
2. For seminal work on the practical, readers should consult H. Garfinkel *Studies in Ethnomethodology*, (Prentice Hall, Englewood Cliffs, 1967).
3. Department of Education and Science, Administrative Memorandum 15/77, Health Education in Schools (HMSO, London, 1977).
4. The Schools Council, Health Education Project, *Think Well*, 5-13, (Nelson, London, 1977), Introduction and Planning booklet, p. 4.
5. Ibid., p. 5.
6. Ibid., p. 6.
7. From D.C. Anderson, 'Curriculum Innovation and Local Need', *Journal of Curriculum Studies*, Vol. 11, No. 2, pp. 118-19.

8. Garfinkel, *Studies*.

9. An expression of Garfinkel's.

10. M Eraut *et al*, 'The Analysis of Curriculum Materials', University of Sussex, Education Area Paper No. 2.

11. D.C. Anderson and W.W. Sharrock, 'Irony as a Methodological Convenience' in E.L. Wright (ed.), *Irony*, (Harvester Press, 1980, in press).

12. Transcript notation given at the end of these notes.

13. H. Sacks, Lectures at the University of California at Irvine and Los Angeles, (1968-72).

14. M. Macdonald Ross, 'Behavioural Objectives – A Critical Review', *Instructional Science*, (1973), 2, pp. 1-52.

15. M.W. Apple, 'The Adequacy of Systems Management Procedures in Education', *Journal of Educational Research*, (1972), 66, pp. 10-18.

16. H. Sacks, Lecture on Topic, University of California, (April 17, 1968).

17. The above description of classroom lessons is a slightly abused version of D.C. Anderson, 'The Formal Basis for a Contextually Sensitive Classroom Agenda', *Instructional Science* (1979), 8, pp. 43-65.

18. Schools Council, *Health Education*, Introductory and Planning Booklet, pp. 3-4.

19. P:C., W.W. Sharrock, University of Manchester.

20. Schools Council, *Health Education*, Food for Thought, pp. 5-7.

21. From D.C. Anderson, 'The Classroom as a Context in Health Education', in D.C. Anderson (ed.), *Health Education in Practice*, (Croom Helm, 1979), pp. 152-7.

22. See D.C. Anderson, 'Systematic and Modest Schemes for Health Education in Schools' in D.C. Anderson (ed.), *The Ignorance of Social Intervention*, (Croom Helm, London, 1980).

## Data Appendix

*Transcription Symbols*

| | |
|---|---|
| * | syllable in a name – omitted for anonymity |
| – | pause of less than a second |
| 0.4 | four second pause |
| ( ) | something said but transcriber cannot discern it |
| (heart) | transcriber thinks that 'heart' was said |
| ([laughter]) | description not transcription |
| —— | underlining indicates emphasis |
| = | indicates latching – one word starts immediately on conclusion of another |
| TV, A, TB, C Mr K, HE, TC | teachers |
| P | pupil |
| . . . | omission from text |

Figures in margin indicate utterance number.

Anderson, D.C., 'Borrowing Other Peoples' Facts', paper given at the
    British Sociological Association Annual Conference, University of
    Warwick (1979); 'Curriculum Innovation and Local Need', *Journal
    of Curriculum Studies*, Vol. 11, No. 2, (1979), pp. 117-23;
    *Evaluation by Classroom Experience* (Nafferton Books, Driffield,
    1979); (ed.), *Health Education in Practice*, (Croom Helm, London,
    1979); 'Literary and Rhetorical Features in the Local Organisation
    of Sociological Arguments' (unpublished PhD thesis, Brunel
    University, 1977); 'Some Organisational Features in the Local
    Production of a Plausible Text', *Philosophy of the Social Sciences*,
    Vol. 8, No. 2, (1978), pp. 113-35; (ed.), *Social Intervention and
    Ignorance*, (Croom Helm, London, 1980); 'Social Work Reports
    and the Grammar of Organisational Reaction', *Analytic Sociology*,
    Vol. No. 3, (1978); 'Stories and Arguments', *Pragmatics Microfiche*,
    PM 3:1:E9 (1978); 'The Formal Basis for a Contextually Sensitive
    Classroom Agenda', *Instructional Science*, Vol. 8, No. 2, (1979),
    pp. 43-65; 'Curricular as Implicative Descriptions of Classrooms',
    Occasional Paper No. 11, Leverhulme Health Education Project
    (Nottingham University, 1978)
— and Sharrock, W.W., 'A Sociology of Directional Hospital Signs',
    in *The Information Design Journal*, Vol. No. 2, (1979); 'Biasing
    the News: Technical Issues in Media Analysis', *Sociology*, Vol. 13,
    No. 3, (1979), pp. 367-85; 'On the Use of Illustrated Ideology as a
    Method for Analysing the Media', in M. Cain and J. Finch, *From
    Epistemology to Methods*, forthcoming; 'Irony as a Methodological
    Convenience', in E.L. Wright, *Irony*, (Harvester, 1980)
Apple, M.W. 'The Adequacy of Systems Management Procedures in
    Education', *Journal of Educational Research*, No. 66, (1972),
    pp. 10-18
Aristotle, *The 'Art' of Rhetoric*, translated by J.H. Freese, (LCL,
    1926)
Bell, C. *Inside the Whale: Ten Personal Accounts of Social Research*,
    (Pergamon, London, 1978)
Bobrow, D. and Collins, A. *Representations and Understandings in
    Cognitive Sciences*, (Academic Press, New York, 1975)
Boden, M.A. *Piaget*, (Fontana Collins, Glasgow, 1979)
Booth, W. *The Rhetoric of Fiction*, (University of Chicago Press,
    Chicago, 1961)

Coulter, J. 'Harvey Sacks: A Preliminary Appreciation', *Sociology*,
    Vol. 10, (1976), pp. 507-12
Cicourel, A.V. *Method and Measurement in Sociology*, (Free Press,
    New York, 1964)
— *et al*, *Language Use and School Performance*, (Academic Press,
    New York, 1974)
Dixon, P. *Rhetoric*, (Methuen, London, 1971)
Donaldson, M. *Children's Minds*, (Fontana Collins, Glasgow, 1978)
Eraut, M. *et al*, 'The Analysis of Curriculum Materials', University
    of Sussex Area Occasional Paper No. 2
Garfinkel, H. *Studies in Ethnomethodology*, (Prentice Hall, Englewood
    Cliffs, 1967)
— and H. Sacks, 'On the Formal Structures of Practical Actions', in
    J.C. McKinney and E.A. Tiryakian (eds), *Theoretical Sociology:
    Perspectives and Developments*, (Appleton-Century Crofts, New
    York, 1970)
Gumperz, J.J. and Hymes, D. *Directions in Sociolinguistics: The
    Ethnography of Communication*, (Holt, Rinehart and Winston,
    1970)
Huff, D. *How to Lie with Statistics*, (Penguin, London, 1973)
Holsti, O. *Content Analysis for the Social Sciences and Humanities*,
    (Addison Wesley, 1969)
Macdonald Ross, M. 'Behavioural Objectives: A Critical Review',
    *Instructional Science*, Vol. 2, (1973), pp. 1-52
McKinney, J.C. and Tiryakian, E.A. (eds), *Theoretical Sociology:
    Perspectives and Development*, (Appleton-Century Crofts, New
    York, 1970)
Munro, R.G. *Innovation: Success or Failure?*, (Hodder and Stoughton,
    London, 1977)
Murdock, G. and Phelps, G. Schools Council Research Study, *Mass
    Media and the Secondary School* (Macmillan, London, 1973)
Parlett, M. and Hamilton, D. 'Evaluation as Illumination: A New
    Approach to the Study of Innovatory Programs', Centre for
    Research and Education Sciences, University of Edinburgh,
    Occasional Paper No. 9
Richards, I.A. *The Philosophy of Rhetoric*, (Oxford University Press,
    New York, 1965)
Rummelhart, D. 'Notes on a Scheme for Stories', in Bobrow and
    Collins (eds), *Representational Understanding*
Sacks, H. 'An Initial Investigation of the Usability of Conversational
    Data for Doing Sociology', in D. Sudnow, *Studies in Social*

*Interaction*, 'On the Analysability of Stories by Children', in Gumperz and Hymes, *Directions*; 'Sociological Description', *Berkeley Journal of Sociology*, 8, (1963), Lectures, University of California at Los Angeles, Berkeley and Irvine

Schegloff, E.A. 'Notes on a Conversational Practice: Formulating Place', in Sudnow (ed), *Studies in Social Interaction*

Schools Council, *Moral Education in the Secondary School*, (Longman, London, 1972); *Health Education Project 5-13*, (Nelson, London, 1977); *Religious Education in Primary Schools: Discovering an Approach*, (Macmillan, London, 1977); *Mass Media and the Secondary School*, (Macmillan, London, 1973)

Schools Council/Nuffield Humanities Project, *The Humanities Project, an Introduction*, (Heinemann, London, 1970)

School and Society, E283, Open University Course

Schwab, J. 'The Practical – a Language for Curriculum', *School Review*, Vol. 78, No. 1, (1969)

Smith, D. 'K is Mentally Ill: the Anatomy of a Factual Account', *Sociology*, Vol. 12, No. 1, (1978)

Sudnow, D. *Studies in Social Interaction*, (Free Press, New York, 1972)

Tarski, A. *Logic, Semantics and Metamathematics*, Papers 1923-38, (Oxford University Press, London, 1969)

Turner, R. (ed.), *Ethnomethodology*, (Penguin, Harmondsworth, 1974)

Wright, E.L. (ed.), *Irony*, (Harvester, 1980)

Young, M.F.D. (ed.), *Knowledge and Control*, (Collier-Macmillan, London, 1971)

# INDEX